CliffsTestPrep®
Regents Integrated Algebra Workbook

An American BookWorks Corporation Project

Contributing Authors

Flavia Banu
Bayside High School
Bayside, New York

Kevin Pendergast
Binghamton High School
Binghamton, New York

Lauren Tallarine
Hauppauge High School
Hauppauge, New York

WILEY

Wiley Publishing, Inc.

Publisher's Acknowledgments

Editorial

Project Editor: Kelly Dobbs Henthorne

Acquisition Editor: Greg Tubach

Production

Proofreader: Laura L. Bowman

Wiley Publishing, Inc. Composition Services

CliffsTestPrep® Regents Integrated Algebra Workbook

Published by:
Wiley Publishing, Inc.
111 River Street
Hoboken, NJ 07030-5774
www.wiley.com

Published by Wiley, Hoboken, NJ
Published simultaneously in Canada

Library of Congress Cataloging-in-Publication data is available from the publisher upon request.
ISBN: 978-0-470-16782-3
Printed in the United States of America
10 9 8 7 6 5 4 3 2

Table of Contents

Introduction

About This Book

The New York State Integrated Algebra Regents Examination is a brand-new test and a brand-new course. It is not the same algebra test that was given 30 years ago. The basis of this course is the algebra *content strand*. Because algebra provides tools and ways of thinking that are necessary for solving problems in a wide variety of disciplines, such as science, business, social sciences, fine arts, and technology, this new course/exam has been built around that concept. This course will assist you in developing skills and processes to be applied using various techniques to successfully solve problems in a variety of settings.

In order to make your studying more effective and help you prepare for a test that has no previous Regents Examinations from which you can study, our authors—all New York State Mathematics teachers—have compiled hundreds of questions (along with fully explained answers) from past mathematics exams that are appropriate for this new exam. We have created a unique book for you that will help you prepare for this exam in a logical manner. Why is it unique? Instead of presenting pages and pages of review material, like most other test preparation books, this book (and the accompanying series) focuses solely on the test questions themselves. It has long been accepted that the more you practice on the types of questions that will appear on the actual examination, the better you will do on the final test, and in that vein, we have provided hundreds of practice questions.

To present these questions in a logical manner, we've divided the book into chapters based on the *types* of questions that you will find on the actual Integrated Algebra Exam. You will find all of the questions that are the same major topic in a chapter together so that you can practice answering them as you go along. We've also provided the explanatory answers following each question to help reinforce your knowledge. Read the question, answer it to the best of your ability, and then *immediately* check the answer to see whether it's correct. We've tried to focus on the correct answers here, although when a question might be somewhat confusing, we've also explained why the other answers are incorrect. In most instances the correct answers are factual, and therefore, if you get the correct answer, there is no need to explain why the other answers are incorrect. After all, as the saying goes, two plus two is always four. In the open-response questions, we've explained the answers in clear, understandable terms.

We've divided the book into five major sections/topics based on the requirements of the actual exam. Within each topic, we've also included the subtopics that are normally covered on the exam, and you will find each answer coded by this subtopic. By using these subtopics, you can quickly determine where you need additional help. Following are the five major sections of the book, including the covered subtopics.

Number Sense and Operations
  Number Systems
  Number Theory
  Operations
  Estimation

Algebra

Variables and Expressions

Equations and Inequalities

Patterns, Relations, and Functions

Coordinate Geometry

Trigonometric Functions

Geometry

Shapes

Geometric Relationships

Transformational Geometry

Coordinate Geometry

Constructions

Locus

Informal Proofs

Formal Proofs

Measurement

Units of Measurement

Tools and Methods

Units

Error and Magnitude

Estimation

Statistics and Probability

Collection of Data

Organization and Display of Data

Analysis of Data

Predictions from Data

Probability

As you go through the book, it's up to you to answer the question before you look at the answers. You're "on your honor" to test yourself. There's no grade at the end, of course, so if you look at the answers first, you're only cheating yourself. You will want to practice answering as many of the test questions as possible.

Organization of the Test and Scoring

As of this writing it is anticipated that there will be a total of 39 questions on the new exam, and they will be broken down by topic and percentage of coverage as follows:

1. Number Sense and Operations: 6–10%
2. Algebra: 50–55%
3. Geometry: 14–19%
4. Measurement: 3–8%
5. Probability and Statistics: 14–19%

There will be 30 multiple-choice questions and 9 open-ended questions. Of these open-ended questions, they will be scored as follows:

3 open-ended questions worth 2 credits each

3 open-ended questions worth 3 credits each

3 open-ended questions worth 4 credits each

That's a total score of 57, which is the raw score, which then will be converted into a standard score. Naturally, the better your raw score is, the better your standard score will be.

The Multiple-Choice Format

Most of the standardized tests that you've probably taken throughout your educational career have contained multiple-choice questions. For some reason, these types of questions give a large percentage of test takers a difficult time. If you approach these questions carefully, they are easier than you think. Considering that at least half of your score on this exam is based on multiple-choice questions, it makes sense to understand how to answer them to the best of your ability.

Let's analyze the concept of the multiple-choice question. Keep in mind that these questions are created to test your abilities to recognize the correct answer from four choices, at least on this specific exam. Other tests may have more or fewer choices.

Questions are comprised of several parts:

- The question stem
- The correct choice
- Distracters

As test-item writers create questions, they normally approach it as follows:

- One choice is absolutely correct.
- One or two choices are absolutely incorrect (distracters).
- One or two choices may be similar to the correct answer, but might contain some information that is not quite accurate or on target, or even might not answer the specific question (distracters).

How do you approach these questions? First, read the question and see whether you know the answer. If you know it automatically, then you can look at the choices and select the correct one. But keep in mind that the answers to the multiple-choice questions on the Integrated Algebra exam are based on the information given in the question. Just focus on the question and don't bring in any outside information. If you understand mathematics, you should have an easy time solving these problems.

One point of interest: A graphing calculator is permitted but not required for this examination.

If the answer does not come to mind quickly, or you're having trouble doing the calculations, the easiest way to answer a multiple-choice question is the time-honored approach of *process of elimination*—especially if you don't know the answer right from the start.

You start by eliminating choices that do not seem logical, or those that you know immediately are incorrect. If you can start by eliminating one of those choices, you now have only three choices left. You've improved your odds of selecting the correct answer from one out of four (25 percent) to one out of three (33⅓ percent), which is a lot better.

Can you eliminate another answer choice? Perhaps one doesn't sound quite right, or it doesn't seem to pertain to the passage you just read. If you can eliminate another choice, you've increased your odds to one out of two (50 percent).

Now, unless you know the correct answer, you can guess.

Pay attention to words like *always*, *never*, or *not*. Most things in the world are not *always* or *never*, and you should be careful if a question asks you to choose which of the choices is NOT . . .! Watch the wording also on questions that state "All are correct EXCEPT . . .!" Make sure you also pay attention to the format of the questions and required answers—are they asking for centimeters or inches, pounds or grams, fractions or decimals, and so on.

The Open-Ended Format

The open-response questions appear in many forms throughout Parts II, III, and IV. We have tried to present a wide-range of these questions so that you'll be prepared for any eventuality. You will be asked to draw illustrations and perform calculations. There will be graphs or charts to develop. But most important, please read the directions for each question very carefully. The questions will specify *how* the answer is to be expressed, whether it is solving a series of equations graphically, or you are asked to find the answer to the "nearest tenth of a foot." You may be given a problem with the degrees expressed in Fahrenheit, but asked to convert your answer to Centigrade. If you don't follow the instructions to the letter, you will lose credits.

The Integrated Algebra exam should not be difficult, since you've been studying this material all year. As long as you read carefully and follow the instructions throughout—and most important—understand the questions and what is being asked of you, you should be able to do well on the exam. Practice answering all of the questions in the book to become familiar with the style and approach that you'll find on the actual exam. Check your answers as you go through the material. Try to determine what needs further study. The wealth of questions and answers presented here represent almost all of the material that you've studied throughout the year and should serve as an ideal review of the subject.

Finally, take the practice test at the end of the book and again, check your answers. It's the best way to evaluate how far you've come and how prepared you are for the actual test. Don't panic if you had problems with this test. Go back to the subjects and reread the earlier questions in the appropriate chapters. If you still don't understand the material, check your textbook, or ask your teacher.

The Regents Examination in Integrated Algebra will include a reference sheet that contains formulas for trigonometric ratios, area, volume, surface area, and coordinate geometry. The reference sheet that follows this introduction can be torn out and used while going through the various practice questions. These formulas also are included on a reference sheet at the beginning of the practice test at the end of this book.

Remember that the more you practice, the better you will do on your actual test. But now it's time to start working. Good luck!

Algebra Reference Sheet

The Regents Examination in Integrated Algebra will include a reference sheet containing the formulas specified here. You also will need this reference sheet while going through the practice questions and the self-evaluation test.

Trigonometric Ratios	$\sin A = \dfrac{opposite}{hypotenuse}$
	$\cos A = \dfrac{adjacent}{hypotenuse}$
	$\tan A = \dfrac{opposite}{hypotenuse}$

| Area | trapezoid | $A = \frac{1}{2}h(b_1+b_2)$ |

| Volume | cylinder | $V = \pi r^2 h$ |

| Surface Area | rectangular prism | $SA = 2lw + 2hw + 2lh$ |
| | cylinder | $SA = 2\pi r^2 + 2\pi rh$ |

| Formulas for Coordinate Geometry | $m = \dfrac{\Delta y}{\Delta x} = \dfrac{y_2 - y_1}{x_2 - x_1}$ |
| | $M = \left(\dfrac{x_1 + x_2}{2} , \dfrac{y_1 + y_2}{2}\right)$ |

Number Sense

Multiple-Choice Questions

1. Jeremy's bedroom has two doors leading into the hallway. His house has four doors leading to the outside. Using the doorways, in how many different ways can Jeremy leave his room and go outside?

   (1) 8
   (2) 6
   (3) 5
   (4) 4

Correct Answer: (1) 8. To answer this question, use the Counting Principle. In this problem, multiply the number of doors leading to the hall by the number of doors leading to the outside, and that is $2 \times 4 = 8$. *(Operations)*

2. Which expression is equivalent to x^{-4}?

   (1) $\dfrac{1}{x^4}$
   (2) x^4
   (3) $-4x$
   (4) 0

Correct Answer: (1) $\dfrac{1}{x^4}$. Change the base to its reciprocal and then rewrite the exponent as a positive. Do not move the coefficient. *(Operations)*

3. Which number is irrational?

   (1) $\sqrt{9}$
   (2) $\sqrt{8}$
   (3) 0.3333
   (4) $\dfrac{2}{3}$

Correct Answer: (2) $\sqrt{8}$. This number is irrational because its value is a non-repeating, non-terminating decimal. *(Number Systems)*

---

4. The amount of time, t, in seconds, it takes an object to fall a distance, d, in meters, is expressed by the formula $t = \sqrt{\dfrac{d}{4.9}}$. Approximately how long will it take an object to fall 75 meters?

   (1) 0.26 sec

   (2) 2.34 sec

   (3) 3.9 sec

   (4) 7.7 sec

Correct Answer: (3) 3.9 sec. Since d represents the distance an object falls and it's given that the object falls 75 meters, plug 75 in for d and solve for t. Use a calculator. *(Operations)*

---

5. At the beginning of her mathematics class, Mrs. Reno gives a warm-up problem. She says, "I am thinking of a number such that 6 less than the product of 7 and this number is 85." Which number is she thinking of?

   (1) 11

   (2) 13

   (3) 84

   (4) 637

Correct Answer: (2) 13. Try each choice. $7(13) - 6 = 85$. So choice (2) works.

Incorrect Choices: $7(11) - 6 \neq 85$, so choice (1) does not work. $7(84) - 6 \neq 85$, so choice (3) does not work. $7(637) - 6 \neq 85$, so choice (4) does not work. *(Operations)*

---

6. If $x^3 < x < \dfrac{1}{x}$, then x could be equal to

   (1) 1

   (2) 5

   (3) $\dfrac{6}{5}$

   (4) $\dfrac{1}{5}$

Correct Answer: (4) $\dfrac{1}{5}$. For 1 over x to be larger then x, x would have to be less than 1, but not equal to zero. *(Operations)*

7. Which equation illustrates the distributive property?

   (1) $5(a + b) = 5a + 5b$
   (2) $a + b = b + a$
   (3) $a + (b + c) = (a + b) + c$
   (4) $a + 0 = a$

Correct Answer: (1) $5(a + b) = 5a + 5b$. Using the distributive property means to take an expression, in this case, 5, that is being multiplied by a quantity in a set of parentheses $(a + b)$, and multiply it by each expression in the parentheses. *(Number Systems)*

8. If M and A represent integers, $M + A = A + M$ is an example of which property?

   (1) commutative
   (2) associative
   (3) distributive
   (4) closure

Correct Answer: (1) commutative. The commutative property of addition states that you can change the order in which numbers are added without affecting the sum. The associative property says that you can group three numbers differently without affecting their sum, such as $A + (B + C) = (A + B) + C$. The distributive property combines the operations of multiplication and addition such as $a(b + c) = ab + ac$. Closure says that within a set of numbers and for a certain operation, an answer remains in that particular set of numbers. For example, when you add two integers, your answer will always be another integer. *(Number Systems)*

9. The number $1.56 \blacklozenge 10^{-2}$ is equivalent to

   (1) 156
   (2) 0.156
   (3) 0.0156
   (4) 0.00156

Correct Answer: (3) 0.0156. The -2 power tells us to move the decimal point 2 units left. *(Operations)*

10. The mass of an orchid seed is approximately 0.0000035 gram. Written in scientific notation, that mass is equivalent to $3.5 \times 10n$. What is the value of n?

   (1) -8
   (2) -7
   (3) -6
   (4) -5

Correct Answer: (3) -6. To get from 3.5 to 0.0000035, you have to move the decimal to the left 6 places so n is the number of places you move the decimal, and if you move to the left, then n is negative. *(Operations)*

11. Which statement is logically equivalent to the statement "If you <u>are</u> an elephant, then you do <u>not</u> forget"?

    (1) If you do not forget, then you are an elephant.
    (2) If you do <u>not</u> forget, then you are <u>not</u> an elephant.
    (3) If you are an elephant, then you forget.
    (4) If you forget, then you are not an elephant.

Correct Answer: (4) If you forget, then you are not an elephant. The phrase logically equivalent indicates that the answer should be the contrapostive. The contrapositive switches and negates the two parts of the statement. *(Operations)*

12. Which property of real numbers is illustrated by the equation $-\sqrt{3} + \sqrt{3} = 0$?

    (1) additive identity
    (2) commutative property of addition
    (3) associative property of addition
    (4) additive inverse

Correct Answer: (4) additive inverse. The additive inverse of a given number is the number that when added to the given number yields the additive identity, 0. *(Number Systems)*

13. A cake recipe calls for 1.5 cups of milk and 3 cups of flour. Seth made a mistake and used 5 cups of flour. How many cups of milk should he use to keep the proportions correct?

    (1) 1.75
    (2) 2
    (3) 2.25
    (4) 2.5

Correct Answer: (4) 2.5. Set up a proportion to solve this such as $\frac{1.5}{3} = \frac{n}{5}$, where n = cups of milk. Set the product of one diagonal (15×5) equal to the product of the other diagonal ($3 \times n$) and solve to get $n = 2.5$. *(Operations)*

14. Cole's Ice Cream Stand serves sixteen different flavors of ice cream, three types of syrup, and seven types of sprinkles. If an ice cream sundae consists of one flavor of ice cream, one type of syrup, and one type of sprinkles, how many different ice cream sundaes can Cole serve?

   (1) 10,836

   (2) 336

   (3) 3

   (4) 26

Correct Answer: (2) 336. Using the Counting Principle, multiply the number of flavors, number of syrups, and number of sprinkles together ($16 \cdot 3 \cdot 7$) to get 336, the number of different ice cream sundaes that can be made. *(Operations)*

15. What is the multiplicative inverse of $\frac{3}{4}$?

   (1) -1

   (2) $\frac{4}{3}$

   (3) $-\frac{4}{3}$

   (4) $-\frac{3}{4}$

Correct Answer: (2) $\frac{4}{3}$. The multiplicative inverse is the reciprocal of the number, and $\frac{4}{3}$ is the reciprocal of $\frac{3}{4}$. *(Number Theory)*

16. The expression $\sqrt{50} + \sqrt{32}$ is equivalent to

   (1) $9\sqrt{2}$

   (2) $\sqrt{82}$

   (3) 6

   (4) 18

Correct Answer: (1) $9\sqrt{2}$. First simplify each radical, $\sqrt{50} = 5\sqrt{2}$ and $\sqrt{32} = 4\sqrt{2}$. Now add the radicals together because they're like radicals and get $9\sqrt{2}$. *(Operations)*

17. What is the value of $3^0 + 3^{-2}$?

  (1) 0

  (2) $\frac{1}{9}$

  (3) $1\frac{1}{9}$

  (4) 6

Correct Answer: (3) $1\frac{1}{9}$. You can enter this entire expression into your calculator to get the correct answer. Otherwise, recall that anything to the zero power equals one. Negative powers ask us to take the reciprocal of the same positive power. So, $3^{-2} = \frac{1}{3^2}$ or $\frac{1}{9}$. $1 + \frac{1}{9}$ is choice (3). *(Operations)*

18. The statement "x is *not* the square of an integer, and x is a multiple of 3" is true when x is equal to

  (1) 9

  (2) 18

  (3) 32

  (4) 36

Correct Answer: (2) 18. The numbers in choices (2) and (3) are not squares of an integer. The number in choice 2 is a multiple of 3 since 6(3) = 18. *(Number Theory)*

19. If $r = 2$ and $s = -7$, what is the value of $|r| - |s|$?

  (1) 5

  (2) –5

  (3) 9

  (4) –9

Correct Answer: (2) –5. Evaluate the absolute value of r, which equals 2 and the absolute value of s, which equals 7 and subtract 2 – 7 to get –5. *(Operations)*

20. The expression $-|-7|$ is equivalent to

  (1) 1

  (2) 0

  (3) 7

  (4) –7

Correct Answer: (4) –7. The first step is to take the absolute value of –7, which is 7, and then multiply it by the negative outside the absolute value and obtain –7. *(Operations)*

21. Which equation illustrates the associative property of addition?

   (1) $x + y = y + x$
   (2) $3(x + 2) = 3x + 6$
   (3) $(3 + x) + y = 3 + (x + y)$
   (4) $3 + x = 0$

Correct Answer: (3) $(3 + x) + y = 3 + (x + y)$. The associative property of addition states that if more than two numbers are added, the order in which they are added does not matter. *(Operations)*

22. On a scale drawing of a new school playground, a triangular area has sides with lengths of 8 centimeters, 15 centimeters, and 17 centimeters. If the triangular area located on the playground has a perimeter of 120 meters, what is the length of its longest side?

   (1) 24 m
   (2) 40 m
   (3) 45 m
   (4) 51 m

Correct Answer: (4) 51 m. First, find the perimeter of the triangle in the scale drawing and then set up a proportion comparing the longest side and perimeter of the scale drawing to the longest side and perimeter of the actual triangle, such as $\frac{17}{40} = \frac{n}{120}$ and solve for *n*. *(Operations)*

23. Rashawn bought a CD that cost $18.99 and paid $20.51, including sales tax. What was the rate of the sales tax?

   (1) 5%
   (2) 2%
   (3) 3%
   (4) 8%

Correct Answer: (4) 8%. $20.51 – $18.99 = $1.52, the amount of money spent on tax. Sales tax is $\frac{1.52}{18.99} = 0.08 = 8\%$. *(Operations)*

24. Which expression has the *smallest* value?

   (1) $-\pi$
   (2) $-\sqrt{10}$
   (3) $\frac{-16}{5}$
   (4) -3.02

Correct Answer: (3) $\frac{-16}{5}$. Using a calculator, convert each choice into a decimal equivalent, and since all the choices are negative, the correct answer would be one with the largest absolute value. That is choice 3. *(Number Theory)*

25. If a and b are both odd integers, which expression must always equal an odd integer?

   (1) $a + b$

   (2) $a - b$

   (3) $a \cdot b$

   (4) $\dfrac{a}{b}$

Correct Answer: (3) $a \cdot b$. If you can't remember the rule that the product of two odd integers is an odd integer, then an effective way to answer this question is to plug in odd integers for a and b into the choices. If you pick $a = 3$ and $b = 5$, then choices 1 and 2 result in an even integer, choice 3 is not an integer, and choice 3 results in an odd integer. *(Number Theory)*

26. The multiplicative inverse of $-\dfrac{1}{3}$ is

   (1) $\dfrac{1}{3}$

   (2) $-\dfrac{1}{3}$

   (3) 3

   (4) -3

Correct Answer: (4) -3. When a number and its multiplicative inverse are multiplied, the result is the multiplicative identity of one. A number multiplied by its reciprocal equals one. The reciprocal of $-\dfrac{1}{3}$ is -3. In equation form, $-\dfrac{1}{3}x = 1$. Choice (4), -3, satisfies this equation. *(Number Systems)*

27. The value of $\dfrac{7!}{3!}$ is

   (1) 840

   (2) 24

   (3) 7

   (4) 4

Correct Answer: (1) 840. Plug this expression into a calculator or do $\dfrac{7 \cdot 6 \cdot 5 \cdot 4 \cdot 3 \cdot 2 \cdot 1}{3 \cdot 2 \cdot 1}$ to get 840. *(Operations)*

28. When $\sqrt{72}$ is expressed in simplest $a\sqrt{b}$ form, what is the value of a?

   (1) 6

   (2) 2

   (3) 3

   (4) 8

Correct Answer: (1) 6. To simplify radicals, find the largest perfect square factor. In this case, the largest perfect square factor is 36, so $\sqrt{72} = \sqrt{36} \cdot \sqrt{2} = 6\sqrt{2}$. Since a is the number outside the radical, a is 6. *(Operations)*

29. Which expression is an example of the associative property?

   (1) $(x + y) + z = x + (y + z)$
   (2) $x + y + z = z + y + x$
   (3) $x(y + z) = xy + xz$
   (4) $x \cdot 1 = x$

Correct Answer: (1) $(x + y) + z = x + (y + z)$. Associativity states that when more than two numbers are added, they can be added in pairs regardless of order. *(Number Theory)*

30. The equation $\clubsuit(\Delta + \heartsuit) = \clubsuit\Delta + \clubsuit\heartsuit$ is an example of the

   (1) associative law
   (2) commutative law
   (3) distributive law
   (4) transitive law

Correct Answer: (3) distributive law. The distributive law means to take an expression that is being multiplied by a set of parentheses (the left of the equation) and that expression is multiplied by every term inside the parentheses to get the right side of the equation. *(Number Theory)*

31. If the mass of a proton is 1.67×10^{-24} gram, what is the mass of 1,000 protons?

   (1) 1.67×10^{-24}g
   (2) 1.67×10^{-23}g
   (3) 1.67×10^{-22}g
   (4) 1.67×10^{-21}g

Correct Answer: (4) 1.67×10^{-21}g. $1.67 \times 10^{-24} \times 1000 = 1.67 \times 10^{-24} \times 10^3 = 1.67 \times 10^{-21}$. *(Operations)*

32. The height of a golf ball hit into the air is modeled by the equation $h = -16t^2 + 48t$, where h represents the height, in feet, and t represents the number of seconds that have passed since the ball was hit. What is the height of the ball after 2 seconds?

   (1) 16 ft.
   (2) 32 ft.
   (3) 64 ft.
   (4) 80 ft.

Correct Answer: (2) 32 ft. Since t represents time and 2 is given for time, plug 2 in for t $(-16(2)^2 + 48(2))$ and solve for h, which equals 32 feet. *(Operations)*

33. The expression 0.62×10^3 is equivalent to

    (1) 0.062

    (2) 62,000

    (3) 6.2×10^4

    (4) 6.2×10^2

Correct Answer: (4) 6.2×10^2. In numeric form, the problem is 620, which is not choice 1 or choice 2. Choice 3 written out is 62,000, and choice 4 is 620, so it must be choice 4. *(Operations)*

34. What is the identity element for ♣ in the accompanying table?

♣	r	s	t	u
r	t	r	u	s
s	r	s	t	u
t	u	t	s	r
u	s	u	r	t

    (1) *r*

    (2) *s*

    (3) *t*

    (4) *u*

Correct Answer:(2) *s*. Notice the heading is *r,s,t,u* in that order. Look in the table in which those letters are in that same order down a column and across a row. In column s and row s, the letters are in the same order as the heading. The identity element doesn't change what is given. *(Number Theory)*

35. Which equation illustrates the multiplicative inverse property?

    (1) $1 \cdot x = x$

    (2) $x \cdot \frac{1}{x} = 1$

    (3) $1 \cdot 0 = 0$

    (4) $-1 \cdot x = -x$

Correct Answer: (2) $x \cdot \frac{1}{x} = 1$. The multiplicative inverse property states that a number multiplied by its reciprocal equals 1. *(Number Theory)*

---

36. Which numbers are arranged from smallest to largest?

    (1) $3.14, \frac{22}{7}, \pi, \sqrt{9.1}$

    (2) $\sqrt{9.1}, \pi, 3.14, \frac{22}{7}$.

    (3) $\sqrt{9.1}, 3.14, \frac{22}{7}, \pi$

    (4) $\sqrt{9.1}, 3.14, \pi, \frac{22}{7}$.

Correct Answer: (4) $\sqrt{9.1}, 3.14, \pi, \frac{22}{7}$. Convert the non-decimal numbers to decimals and put the numbers in order. $\sqrt{9.1} = 3.0166, \pi = 3.14159, \frac{22}{7} = 3.14285$. The correct choice is (4). *(Number Theory)*

---

37. What is the first step in simplifying the expression $(2 - 3 \times 4 + 5)^2$?

    (1) square 5
    (2) add 4 and 5
    (3) subtract 3 from 2
    (4) multiply 3 by 4

Correct Answer: (4) multiply 3 by 4. The order of operations states that the operations in the parentheses are performed first. Out of these, multiplication is performed before addition/subtraction. *(Operations)*

---

38. What is the value of 2^{-3}?

    (1) $\frac{1}{6}$

    (2) $\frac{1}{8}$

    (3) -6

    (4) -8

Correct Answer: (2) $\frac{1}{8}$. In this exponent problem, the base is 2 and the exponent is -3. To change an exponent to a positive number, take the reciprocal of the base and your exponent will then be positive. The reciprocal of the base 2 is $\frac{1}{2}$, so the new problem becomes $\left(\frac{1}{2}\right)^3$ and $1^3 = 1$ and $2^3 = 8$ so the answer is choice (2). *(Operations)*

39. Which list shows the numbers $|-0.12|, \sqrt{\frac{1}{82}}, \frac{1}{8}, \frac{1}{9}$ in order from smallest to largest?

   (1) $|-0.12|, \frac{1}{8}, \frac{1}{9}, \sqrt{\frac{1}{82}}$

   (2) $\sqrt{\frac{1}{82}}, |-0.12|, \frac{1}{9}, \frac{1}{8}$

   (3) $\frac{1}{8}, \frac{1}{9}, \sqrt{\frac{1}{82}}, |-0.12|$

   (4) $\sqrt{\frac{1}{82}}, \frac{1}{9}, |-0.12|, \frac{1}{8}$

Correct Answer: (4) $\sqrt{\frac{1}{82}}, \frac{1}{9}, |-0.12|, \frac{1}{8}$

$$|-0.12| = 0.12, \sqrt{\frac{1}{82}} = 0.1104315261, \frac{1}{8} = 0.125, \frac{1}{9} = 0.11111111.$$

The order from smallest to largest is: 0.1104315261, 0.1111111, 0.12, 0.125. *(Operations)*

40. What is an irrational number?

   (1) $0.\overline{3}$

   (2) $\frac{3}{8}$

   (3) $\sqrt{49}$

   (4) π

Correct Answer: (4) π. An irrational number is a number that is a non-terminating and non-repeating decimal. π is a decimal that does not end or repeat. *(Number Theory)*

41. What is the sum of 6×10^3 and 3×10^2?

   (1) 6.3×10^3

   (2) 9×10^5

   (3) 9×10^6

   (4) 18×10^5

Correct Answer: (1) 6.3×10^3. $6 \times 10^3 = 6,000$ and $3 \times 10^2 = 300$ so $6,000 + 300 = 6,300 = 6 \times 10^3$. *(Operations)*

---

42. What is the sum of $5\sqrt{7}$ and $3\sqrt{28}$?

    (1) $9\sqrt{7}$

    (2) $11\sqrt{7}$

    (3) $60\sqrt{7}$

    (4) $8\sqrt{35}$

Correct Answer: (2) $11\sqrt{7}$. In order to add radicals, the radicands must be like. You need to simplify $3\sqrt{28}$, which is $6\sqrt{7}$. Now add the numbers outside the radical and carry over the radical to the answer. So $5\sqrt{7} + 6\sqrt{7} = 11\sqrt{7}$. *(Operations)*

---

43. Expressed in simplest radical form, the product of $\sqrt{6} \cdot \sqrt{15}$ is

    (1) $\sqrt{90}$

    (2) $3\sqrt{10}$

    (3) $9\sqrt{10}$

    (4) $3\sqrt{15}$

Correct Answer: (2) $3\sqrt{10}$. $\sqrt{6} \cdot \sqrt{15} = \sqrt{90} = \sqrt{9} \cdot \sqrt{10} = 3\sqrt{10}$. *(Operations)*

---

44. What is the sum of $\sqrt{50}$ and $\sqrt{32}$?

    (1) $\sqrt{82}$

    (2) $20\sqrt{20}$

    (3) $9\sqrt{2}$

    (4) $\sqrt{2}$

Correct Answer: (3) $9\sqrt{2}$. $\sqrt{50} = \sqrt{25}\sqrt{2} = 5\sqrt{2}$; $\sqrt{32} = \sqrt{16}\sqrt{2} = 4\sqrt{2}$; $\sqrt{50} + \sqrt{32} = 5\sqrt{2} + 4\sqrt{2} = 9\sqrt{2}$. *(Operations)*

---

45. Which statement best illustrates the additive identity property?

    (1) $6 + 2 = 2 + 6$

    (2) $6(2) = 2(6)$

    (3) $6 + (-6) = 0$

    (4) $6 + 0 = 6$

Correct Answer: (4) $6 + 0 = 6$. The additive identity is 0, and it implies that a number plus 0 remains unchanged. *(Number Theory)*

46. Nine hundred students were asked whether they thought their school should have a dress code. A circle graph was constructed to show the results. The central angles for two of the three sectors are shown in the accompanying diagram. What is the number of students who felt that the school should have *no* dress code?

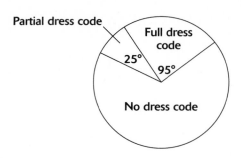

(1) 600
(2) 180
(3) 300
(4) 360

Correct Answer: (1) 600. First find the central angle representing the no dress code. All the central angles in a circle add to 360° and the no dress code is (360 – 95 – 25), which equals 240°. Now set up a proportion to solve for the number of students that you'll let equal n. The proportion is $\frac{240}{360} = \frac{n}{900}$. Solve for n to get 600 students. *(Operations)*

47. If $x = 3$, which statement is *false*?
 (1) x is prime, and x is odd.
 (2) x is odd, or x is even.
 (3) x is not prime, and x is odd.
 (4) x is odd, and $2x$ is even.

Correct Answer: (3) x is not prime, and x is odd. The statement "x is not prime" is false because $x = 3$ is a prime number since it only divides itself and 1. *(Number Theory)*

48. The size of a certain type of molecule is 0.00009078 inch. If this number is expressed as 9.078×10^n, what is the value of n?
 (1) –5
 (2) 5
 (3) –8
 (4) 8

Correct Answer: (1) –5. To rewrite 9.078 as 0.00009078 you need to move the decimal point 5 places to the left, thus the value of n is – 5. *(Operations)*

BLATANT FAUXY.

49. Given the statement: "If x is a rational number, then $\sqrt{x}$ is irrational." Which value of x makes the statement *false*?

(1) $\frac{3}{2}$

(2) 2

(3) 3

(4) 4

Correct Answer: (4) 4. 4 is a rational number, and 2, its square root, is also a rational number. *(Number Systems)*

50. While solving the equation $4(x + 2) = 28$, Becca wrote $4x + 8 = 28$ Which property did she use?

(1) distributive

(2) associative

(3) commutative

(4) identity

Correct Answer: (1) distributive. Becca distributed the 4 on the left side of the equation. *(Number Theory)*

51. Which list is in order from smallest value to largest value?

(1) $\sqrt{10}, \frac{22}{7}, \pi, 3.1$

(2) $3.1, \frac{22}{7}, \pi, \sqrt{10}$

(3) $\pi, \frac{22}{7}, 3.1, \sqrt{10}$

(4) $3.1, \pi, \frac{22}{7}, \sqrt{10}$

Correct Answer: (4) $3.1, \pi, \frac{22}{7}, \sqrt{10}$. $\pi = 3.1415, \frac{22}{7} = 3.1429,$ $\sqrt{10} = 3.1622; 3.1 < 3.1415 < 3.1429 < 3.1622.$ *(Number Systems)*

52. A micron is a unit used to measure specimens viewed with a microscope. One micron is equivalent to 0.00003937 inch. How is this number expressed in scientific notation?

(1) 3.937×10^{-5}

(2) 3.937×10^{5}

(3) 3.937×10^{-8}

(4) 3.937×10^{8}

Correct Answer: (1) 3.937×10^{-5}. The -5 power tells you to move the decimal point to the left 5 places. *(Operations)*

53. Leo purchased five shirts, three pairs of pants, and four pairs of shoes. Which expression represents how many different outfits consisting of one shirt, one pair of pants, and one pair of shoes Leo can make?

(1) $5 \cdot 3 \cdot 4$

(2) $5 + 3 + 4$

(3) $_{12}C_3$

(4) $_{12}P_3$

Correct Answer: (1) $5 \cdot 3 \cdot 4$. By the counting principle, multiply the number of shirts by the number of pairs of pants by the number of pairs of shoes. *(Number Theory)*

54. On February 18, from 9 A.M. until 2 P.M., the temperature rose from $-14°$F to $36°$F. What was the total increase in temperature during this time period?

(1) $50°$

(2) $36°$

(3) $32°$

(4) $22°$

Correct Answer: (1) $50°$. The difference between 36 and -14 is $36 - (-14) = 36 + 14 = 50$. *(Operations)*

55. What is the value of $\frac{8!}{4!}$?

(1) 1,680

(2) 2

(3) 2!

(4) 4!

Correct Answer: (1) 1,680. $\frac{8!}{4!} = \frac{8 \times 7 \times 6 \times 5 \times 4 \times 3 \times 2 \times 1}{4 \times 3 \times 2 \times 1} = 8 \times 7 \times 6 \times 5 = 1,680$. Alternately, use the calculator to evaluate $\frac{8!}{4!}$. *(Number Theory)*

Open-Ended Questions

56. A recent survey shows that the average man will spend 141,288 hours sleeping, 85,725 hours working, 81,681 hours watching television, 9,945 hours commuting, 1,662 hours kissing, and 363,447 hours on other tasks during his lifetime. What percent of his life, to the *nearest tenth of a percent*, does he spend sleeping?

Correct Answer: A man spends 20.7% of his life sleeping. The total number of hours a man lives is $141,288 + 85,725 + 81,681 + 9,945 + 1,662 + 363,447 = 683,748$. The number of hours a man spends sleeping is 141,288, so the percentage of hours he spends sleeping is $\frac{141,288}{683,748} \cdot 100\% \approx 20.7\%$. *(Operations)*

57. Kyoko's mathematics teacher gave her the accompanying cards and asked her to arrange the cards in order from least to greatest. In what order should Kyoko arrange the cards?

$$\boxed{\pi} \quad \boxed{\sqrt{8}} \quad \boxed{3.\overline{1}} \quad \boxed{2\sqrt{3}} \quad \boxed{2\tfrac{4}{5}}$$

Correct Answer: $2\frac{4}{5}, \sqrt{8}, 3.\overline{1}, \pi, 2\sqrt{3}. \ \pi \approx 3.1415, \ \sqrt{8} \approx 2.8284, \ 3.\overline{1} \approx 3.1111, \ 2\sqrt{3} \approx 3.4641,$ $2\frac{4}{5} = 2.8.$ *(Number Systems)*

58. Five friends met for lunch, and they all shook hands. Each person shook the other person's right hand only once. What was the total number of handshakes?

Correct Answer: $_5C_2 = 10$ handshakes. *(Number Theory)*

59. Given: $\dfrac{\sqrt{99}}{11}, \sqrt{164}, \sqrt{196}$

Identify the expression that is a rational number and explain why it is rational.

Correct Answer: $\sqrt{196}$ is rational. All whole numbers are rational, and $\sqrt{196} = 14$, which is a whole number. *(Number Systems)*

60. A car dealer has 22 vehicles on his lot. If 8 of the vehicles are vans and 6 of the vehicles are red, and 10 vehicles are neither vans nor red, how many red vans does he have on his lot?

Correct Answer: There are 2 red vans on the lot.

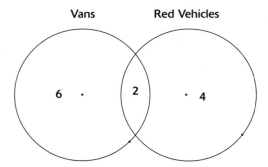

Vans   Red Vehicles

10 Vehicles That Are Neither Vans nor Red

Since 10 vehicles are neither vans nor red, 12 must be red or vans or both. After constructing the Venn diagram, you notice that there are 2 red vans on the lot. *(Number Theory)*

61. In a class of 24 students, 10 have brown hair, 8 have black hair, 4 have blond hair, and 2 have red hair. On the accompanying diagram, construct a circle graph to show the students' hair color.

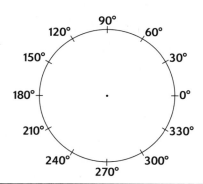

Correct Answer: On the diagram, the brown hair = 150° angle, black hair = 120° angle, blond hair = 60° angle, and red hair = 30°. For each color of hair a proportion could be solved to find out the measure of the angle each color represents, such as (for brown hair, $\frac{10}{24} = \frac{n}{360}$, $n = 150°$). An alternate way would be to look at the diagram and realize that there are 12 equal intervals of 30° each and that each interval represents 2 out of the 24 students, so for brown hair, you would need to draw an angle containing 5 of the intervals. *(Operations)*

62. A 14-gram serving of mayonnaise contains 11 grams of fat. What percent of the mayonnaise, to the *nearest tenth of a percent*, is fat?

Correct Answer: 78.6%. 11 out of 14 grams are fat. 11/14 = .7857142857. You must multiply by 100 or move the decimal to the right two spaces to change your answer to the correct rounded percent of 78.6. *(Operations)*

Algebra

Multiple-Choice Questions

---

1. If $2(x + 3) = x + 10$, then x equals

    (1) 14
    (2) 7
    (3) 5
    (4) 4

Correct Answer: (4) 4. Distribute the 2 on the left side of the equation: $2x + 6 = x + 10$. Subtract 6 and x from both sides: $x = 4$. *(Equations and Inequalities)*

---

2. What is the value of x in the equation $5(2x - 7) = 15x - 10$?

    (1) 1
    (2) 0.6
    (3) -5
    (4) -9

Correct Answer: (3) -5. Distribute the 5 on the left side of the equation: $10x - 35 = 15x - 10$. Subtract $10x$ from each side: $-35 = 5x - 10$. Add 10 to each side: $-25 = 5x$. Divide each side by 5: $-5 = x$. *(Equations and Inequalities)*

---

3. When $3x^2 - 6x$ is divided by $3x$, the result is

    (1) $-2x$
    (2) $2x$
    (3) $x + 2$
    (4) $x - 2$

Correct Answer: (4) $x - 2$. When dividing a polynomial ($3x^2 - 6x$) by a monomial ($3x$), divide each term of the polynomial by the monomial and use the rules of exponents. *(Variables and Expressions)*

4. What is the product of $10x^4y^2$ and $3xy^3$?

    (1) $30x^4y^5$

    (2) $30x^4y^6$

    (3) $30x^5y^5$

    (4) $30x^5y^6$

Correct Answer: (3) $30x^5y^5$. Rearrange the factors since multiplication is commutative. When multiplying two expressions with like bases, add their powers.

$(10x^4y^2)(3xy^3) = (30)(3)(x)^4(x)^1(y)^2(y)^3 = 3x^{4+1}y^{2+3} = 30x^5y^5$. *(Variables and Expressions)*

5. What is the value of x in the equation $13x - 2(x + 4) = 8x + 1$?

    (1) 1

    (2) 2

    (3) 3

    (4) 4

Correct Answer: (3) 3. Distribute -2 on the left side: $13x - 2x - 8 = 8x + 1$. Combine like terms: $11x - 8 = 8x + 1$. Subtract $8x$ from both sides: $3x - 8 = 1$. Add 8 to both sides: $3x = 9$. Divide both sides by 3: $x = 3$. *(Equations and Inequalities)*

6. What is the value of n in the equation $3n - 8 = 32 - n$?

    (1) -10

    (2) -6 $4n = 40$

    (3) 6

    (4) 10

Correct Answer: (4) 10. You must isolate n by combining like terms. Adding n to both sides gives you $4n - 8 = 32$. Adding 8 to both sides gives you $4n = 40$. Dividing both sides by 4 results in $n = 10$. *(Equations and Inequalities)*

7. If $n + 4$ represents an odd integer, the next larger odd integer is represented by

    (1) $n + 2$

    (2) $n + 3$

    (3) $n + 5$

    (4) $n + 6$

Correct Answer: (4) $n + 6$. The next odd integer is 2 more than the first number. So if you start with $n + 4$, then the next is $n + 4 + 2$ or $n + 6$. *(Patterns, Relations, and Functions)*

8. If $7x + 2a = 3x + 5a$, then x is equivalent to

(1) $\dfrac{7a}{10}$

(2) $\dfrac{7a}{4}$

(3) $\dfrac{3a}{10}$

(4) $\dfrac{3a}{4}$

Correct Answer: (4) $\dfrac{3a}{4}$. Get the x terms on one side of the equation and the a terms on the other to get $4x = 3a$. Divide both sides by 4 to get x by itself. *(Equations and Inequalities)*

9. Which expression represents "5 less than the product of 7 and x"?

(1) $7(x - 5)$

(2) $7x - 5$

(3) $7 + x - 5$

(4) $5 - 7x$

$7x - 5$

Correct Answer: (2) $7x - 5$. The product of 7 and x is $7x$. Five less than this product is $7x - 5$.
(Variables and Expressions)

10. What is the value of $\dfrac{x^2 - 4y}{2}$, if $x = 4$ and $y = -3$?

(1) -2

(2) 2

(3) 10

(4) 14

$16 - 4(-3)$

$16 + 12 = \dfrac{28}{2}$

Correct Answer: (4) 14. If $x = 4$ and $y = -3$, then $\dfrac{x^2 - 4y}{2} = \dfrac{(4)^2 - 4(-3)}{2} = \dfrac{16 + 12}{2} = \dfrac{28}{2} = 14$.
(Variables and Expressions)

11. What is the solution set of the equation $x^2 + 11x + 28 = 0$?

(1) $\{-7, 4\}$

(2) $\{-7, -4\}$

(3) $\{3, 4\}$

(4) $\{-3, -4\}$

$(x + 4)(x + 7)$

$x^2 + 7x + 4x \ 28$

Correct Answer: (2) $\{-7, -4\}$. Factor this quadratic equation into $(x + 7)(x + 4) = 0$ and set each factor $= 0$ and solve for x to get $\{-7, -4\}$. *(Equations and Inequalities)*

12. For which value of x will the fraction $\dfrac{3}{2x+4}$ be undefined?

(1) -2
(2) 2
(3) 0
(4) -4

Correct Answer: (1) -2. A fraction is undefined when its denominator is zero. Thus, $2x+4=0$. Subtract 4 from both sides: $2x=-4$. Divide both sides by 2: $x=-2$. *(Equations and Inequalities)*

13. What is the product of $\frac{1}{3}x^2y$ and $\frac{1}{6}xy^3$?

(1) $\frac{1}{2}x^2y^3$

(2) $\frac{1}{9}x^3y^4$

(3) $\frac{1}{18}x^2y^3$

(4) $\frac{1}{18}x^3y^4$

Correct Answer: (4) $\frac{1}{18}x^3y^4$. When multiplying two fractions, multiply the numerators and denominators separately, thus arriving at $\frac{1}{18}$. When multiplying like variables, add the exponents. Thus, $x^2(x)=x^3$ and $y(y^3)=y^4$. *(Variables and Expressions)*

14. The statement $x \geq 4$ and $2x-4 < 6$ is true when x is equal to

(1) 1
(2) 10
(3) 5
(4) 4

Correct Answer: (4) 4. An "and" statement is true whenever both parts of the statement are true. You must solve the second inequality $2x-4 < 6$. Adding 4 to both sides gives you $2x < 10$. Dividing both sides by 2 results in $x < 5$. Therefore, x must be greater than or equal to 4 and also less than 5. Choice (4) is the only value that satisfies both of these criteria. *(Equations and Inequalities)*

15. What is the solution set for the equation $x^2 - 5x + 6 = 0$?

(1) $\{-6, 1\}$
(2) $\{6. 1\}$
(3) $\{-2, -3\}$
(4) $\{2, 3\}$

Correct Answer: (4) $\{2, 3\}$. First factor the equation and get $(x-3)(x-2)=0$; then set each factor equal to zero and solve for x. This gives you 2,3, which is choice 4. *(Equations and Inequalities)*

16. If $x \neq 0$, then $\dfrac{\left(x^2\right)^3}{x^5} \cdot 1000$ is equivalent to

(1) $1000x$ $\dfrac{x^6}{x^5} = x$

(2) $1000 + x$

(3) 1000

(4) 0

Correct Answer: (1) $1000x$. Simplify the first part of the problem using rules of exponents to get $\dfrac{x^6}{x^5} = x$ and multiply x by 1000 to get $1000x$. *(Variable sand Expressions)*

17. The equation $A = \frac{1}{2}(12)(3 + 7)$ is used to find the area of a trapezoid. Which calculation would *not* result in the correct area?

(1) $\dfrac{12\,(3 + 7)}{2}$

(2) $6(3+7)$

(3) $0.5(12)(10)$

(4) $\dfrac{12}{2} \times \dfrac{10}{2}$

Correct Answer: (4) $\dfrac{12}{2} \times \dfrac{10}{2}$. The area of the trapezoid, $\frac{1}{2}(12)(3 + 7)$, can be read as "half of 12, multiplied by 10," which equals 60. All of the choices equal to 60 except for choice (4). *(Variables and Expressions)*

18. If $-2x + 3 = 7$ and $3x + 1 = 5 + y$, the value of y is

(1) 1

(2) 0

(3) -10

(4) 10

Correct Answer: (3) -10. Solve the first equation to get $x = -2$. Plug this into the equation and solve for y to get $y = -10$. *(Equations and Inequalities)*

19. An equation of the line that has a slope of 3 and a y-intercept of -2 is

(1) $x = 3y - 2$

(2) $y = 3x - 2$

(3) $y = -\dfrac{2}{3}x$

(4) $y = -2x + 3$

Correct Answer: (2) $y = 3x - 2$. The slope-intercept form of a line's equation is $y = mx + b$, in which m represents the slope and b represents the y-intercept. *(Patterns, Relations, and Functions)*

20. What is the value of x in the equation $\frac{x}{2x+1} = \frac{4}{3}$?

    (1) $-\frac{1}{5}$

    (2) $-\frac{4}{5}$

    (3) $-\frac{5}{4}$

    (4) -5

Correct Answer: (2) $-\frac{4}{5}$. $\frac{x}{2x+1} = \frac{4}{3}$. Cross-multiply: $3x = 8x + 4$. Subtract $8x$ from both sides: $-5x = 4$. Divide both sides by -5: $x = -\frac{4}{5}$. *(Equations and Inequalities)*

21. The expression $(2x^2 + 6x + 5) - (6x^2 + 3x + 5)$ is equivalent to

    (1) $-4x^2 + 3x$

    (2) $4x^2 - 3x$

    (3) $-4x^2 - 3x + 10$

    (4) $4x^2 + 3x - 10$

Correct Answer: (1) $-4x^2 + 3x$. If you distribute the negative sign to the entire second polynomial, you can rewrite this problem using addition as follows: $(2x^2 + 6x + 5) + (-6x^2 - 3x - 5)$. Now you can combine each pair of like terms.

$2x^2 + -6x^2 = -4x^2$

$6x + -3x = 3x$

$5 + -5 = 0$

Therefore, your final answer is $-4x^2 + 3x$. *(Variables and Expressions)*

22. Which equation represents a line that is parallel to the line whose equation is $2x + 3y = 12$?

    (1) $6y - 4x = 2$

    (2) $6y + 4x = 2$

    (3) $4x - 6y = 2$

    (4) $6x + 4y = -2$

Correct Answer: (2) $6y + 4x = 2$. The first step is to get the given equation in $y = mx + b$ form, which would be $y = -\frac{2}{3}x + 4$. Because parallel lines have the same slope, solving by putting the answers in $y = mx + b$ form shows that Choice 2 also has a slope of $-\frac{2}{3}$. *(Coordinate Geometry)*

23. If point $(-1, 0)$ is on the line whose equation is $y = 2x + b$, what is the value of b?

(1) 1
(2) 2
(3) 3
(4) 0

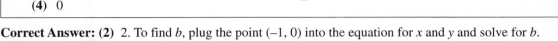

Correct Answer: (2) 2. To find b, plug the point $(-1, 0)$ into the equation for x and y and solve for b. *(Coordinate Geometry)*

24. In order to be admitted for a certain ride at an amusement park, a child must be greater than or equal to 36 inches tall and less than 48 inches tall. Which graph represents these conditions?

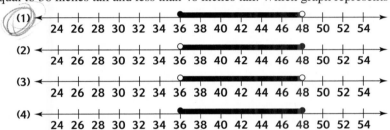

Correct Answer: (1)

Because the child's height could equal 36, 36 must be shaded in; because the child's height cannot be equal to 48, 48 must not be shaded in. *(Equations and Inequalities)*

25. For which value of x is the expression $\dfrac{3}{x - 2}$ undefined?

(1) -2
(2) 2
(3) 3
(4) 0

Correct Answer: (2) 2. A fraction is undefined when its denominator (but not its numerator) is zero. In this case, $x - 2 = 0$ when $x = 2$. *(Patterns, Relations, and Functions)*

26. Which equation represents a line that is perpendicular to the line whose equation is $-2y = 3x + 7$?

    (1) $y = x + 7$

    (2) $2y = 3x - 3$

    (3) $y = \dfrac{2}{3}x - 3$

    (4) $y = \dfrac{3}{2}x - 3$

Correct Answer: (3) $y = \dfrac{2}{3}x - 3$. First find the slope of the given line by putting the equation in $y = mx + b$ form. It is $-\dfrac{3}{2}$. The product of the slopes of two perpendicular lines is -1, so choice 3 has a slope equal to $\dfrac{2}{3}$, which makes the products equal to -1. Another way to look at it is that the slope of a line perpendicular to a given line has a slope equal to the negative reciprocal of the slope of the given line. *(Coordinate Geometry)*

27. When $3a^2 - 7a + 6$ is subtracted from $4a^2 - 3a + 4$, the result is

    (1) $a^2 + 4a - 2$

    (2) $a^2 - 10a - 2$

    (3) $-a^2 - 4a + 2$

    (4) $7a^2 - 10a + 10$

Correct Answer: (1) $a^2 + 4a - 2$. Translating the sentence into algebra, you have $(4a^2 - 3a + 4) - (3a^2 - 7a + 6) = 4a^2 - 3a + 4 - 3a^2 + 7a - 6 = a^2 + 4a - 2$. *(Variables and Expressions)*

28. Which graph best represents the solution set for the inequality $x > \sqrt{2}$?

    (1) -2 -1 0 1 2 3 4 5

    (2) -2 -1 0 1 2 3 4 5

    (3) -2 -1 0 1 2 3 4 5

    (4) -2 -1 0 1 2 3 4 5

Correct Answer: (2)

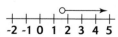

$\sqrt{2} \approx 1.414$; $x > \sqrt{2}$ means all the numbers to the right of 1.414. *(Equations and Inequalities)*

29. Which equation represents the direct variation relationship of the equation $\frac{x}{y} = \frac{1}{2}$?

(1) $y = x + \frac{1}{2}$

(2) $y = 2x$

(3) $y = 3x$

(4) $x = 2y$

Correct Answer: (2) $y = 2x$. Cross-multiplying the original equations results in choice (2). *(Equations and Inequalities)*

30. When $3x^2 - 8x$ is subtracted from $2x^2 + 3x$, the difference is

(1) $-x^2 + 11x$

(2) $x^2 - 11x$

(3) $-x^5 - 5x$

(4) $x^2 - 5x$

Correct Answer: (1) $-x^2 + 11x$. If the problem is set up vertically, the $2x^2 + 3x$ must be on the top. Also important to remember $3x - -8x = 11x$. *(Variables and Expressions)*

31. John left his home and walked 3 blocks to his school, as shown in the accompanying graph.

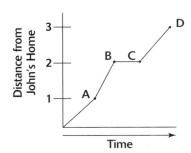

What is one possible interpretation of the section of the graph from point B to point C?

(1) John arrived at school and stayed throughout the day.

(2) John waited before crossing a busy street.

(3) John returned home to get his mathematics homework.

(4) John reached the top of a hill and began walking on level ground.

Correct Answer: (2) John waited before crossing a busy street. The graph from B to C is constant—time goes by but John's distance does not change. This implies that he stopped for some reason. *(Patterns, Relations, and Functions)*

32. In the equation $A = p + prt$, t is equivalent to

(1) $\dfrac{A - pr}{p}$

(2) $\dfrac{A - p}{pr}$

(3) $\dfrac{A}{pr} - p$

(4) $\dfrac{A}{p} - pr$

Correct Answer: (2) $\dfrac{A - p}{pr}$. Here t needs to be isolated. $A = p + prt$. Subtract p from both sides: $A - p = prt$. Divide both sides by pr: $\dfrac{A - p}{pr}$. *(Variables and Expressions)*

33. When $-9x^5$ is divided by $-3x^3$, $x \neq 0$, the quotient is

(1) $-3x^2$

(2) $3x^2$

(3) $-27x^{15}$

(4) $27x^8$

Correct Answer: (2) $3x^2$. $\dfrac{-9x^5}{-3x^3} = 3x^2$. *(Variables and Expressions)*

34. If a line is horizontal, its slope is

(1) 1

(2) 0

(3) undefined

(4) negative

Correct Answer: (2) 0. A horizontal line has 0 slope because all of its points have the same y value, and when the slope formula, $m = \dfrac{y_2 - y_1}{x_2 - x_1}$, is applied to any two points on the line, the numerator (only) will be zero, thus making the value of the fraction zero. *(Patterns, Relations, and Functions)*

35. Which expression represents the product of two consecutive odd integers, where *n* is an odd integer?

(1) $n(n + 1)$
(2) $n(n + 2)$
(3) $n(n + 3)$
(4) $2n + 1$

Correct Answer: (2) $n(n + 2)$. Since odd and even numbers alternate on the number line, the next (consecutive) odd integer would be found by adding 2 to the original number, *n*. This results in $n + 2$. The word product refers to multiplication. This is shown by $n(n + 2)$. *(Variables and Expressions)*

36. Which point is in the solution set of the system of inequalities shown in the accompanying graph?

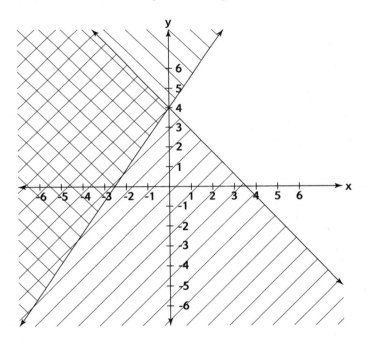

(1) $(0, 4)$
(2) $(2, 4)$
(3) $(-4, 1)$
(4) $(4, -1)$

Correct Answer: (3) $(-4, 1)$. All the points that are solutions will be in the area that is double-shaded. Choice 1 is not correct because although it is the intersection point, one of the lines is dashed so the line is not included in the solution. Choice 3 is the only point in the double-shaded area. *(Coordinate Geometry)*

37. The expression $\dfrac{6\sqrt{20}}{3\sqrt{5}}$ is equivalent to

    (1) $3\sqrt{15}$

    (2) $2\sqrt{15}$

    (3) 8

    (4) 4

Correct Answer: (4) 4. $\dfrac{6\sqrt{20}}{3\sqrt{5}} = 2\sqrt{4} = 2 \cdot 2 = 4$. *(Variables and Expressions)*

38. What is the solution set of the equation $3x^2 - 34x - 24 = 0$?

    (1) $\{-2,6\}$

    (2) $\{-12,\frac{2}{3}\}$

    (3) $\{-\frac{2}{3},12\}$

    (4) $\{-6,2\}$

Correct Answer: (3) $\{-\frac{2}{3},12\}$. When you factor the quadratic of $3x^2 - 34x - 24 = 0$, you get $(3x + 2)(x - 12) = 0$. Then set each factor equal to 0:

$3x + 2 = 0$

$x - 12 = 0$

Subtract 2 from both sides of $3x + 2 = 0$: $3x = -2$. Now divide both sides by 3: $x = \dfrac{-2}{3}$. Add 12 to both sides of $x - 12 = 0$: $x = 12$. *(Equations and Inequalities)*

39. Which point is on the circle whose equation is $x^2 + y^2 = 289$?

    (1) $(-12,12)$

    (2) $(7,-10)$

    (3) $(-1,-16)$

    (4) $(8,-15)$

Correct Answer: (4) $(8,-15)$. Replace the x and y values from each choice into the equation to check which one will give you 289. Choice (4) is the one: $8^2 + (-15)^2 = 289$. *(Patterns, Relations, and Functions)*

40. Chantrice is pulling a wagon along a smooth, horizontal street. The path of the center of one of the wagon wheels (the axle) is best described as

   (1) a circle
   (2) a line perpendicular to the road
   (3) a line parallel to the road
   (4) two parallel lines

Correct Answer: (3) a line parallel to the road. The axle is not rotating but moving horizontally as the wheels rotate. *(Patterns, Relations, and Functions).*

41. Which expression is undefined when $w = 3$?

   (1) $\dfrac{w - 3}{w + 1}$

   (2) $\dfrac{w^2 + 2w}{5w}$

   (3) $\dfrac{w + 1}{w^2 - 3w}$

   (4) $\dfrac{3w}{3w^2}$

Correct Answer: (3) $\dfrac{w + 1}{w^2 - 3w}$. A fraction is considered undefined when its denominator equals zero. You must plug in 3 for w in all of the answer choices. Since $3^2 - 3(3)$ equals 0, choice (3) is undefined for $w = 3$. *(Variables and Expressions)*

42. Expressed in simplest form, $(3x^3)(2y)^2(4x^4)$ is equivalent to

   (1) $24x^{12}y^2$
   (2) $24x^7y^2$
   (3) $48x^{12}y^2$
   (4) $48x^7y^2$

Correct Answer: (4) $48x^7y^2$. The first step is to deal with the y; this is the power to power rule where $(2y)^2 = 4y^2$. Then multiplying all the coefficients yields 48. Keeping both bases and adding the exponents gives choice 4. *(Variables and Expressions)*

43. Which ordered pair is in the solution set of the system of inequalities shown in the accompanying graph?

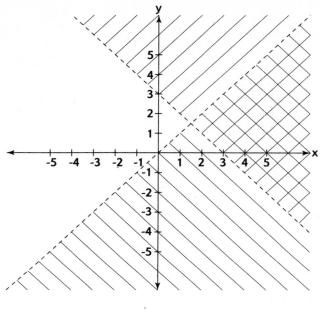

(1) (0,0)

(2) (0,1)

(3) (1,5)

(4) (3,2)

Correct Answer: (4) (3,2). The solution set is the double-shaded region. The point (3,2) is in this region. *(Equations and Inequalities)*

44. Which inequality is represented by the accompanying graph?

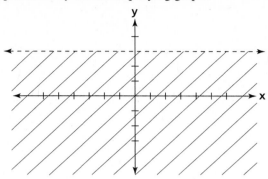

    (1) $y < 3$
    (2) $y > 3$
    (3) $y \leq 3$
    (4) $y \leq 3$

Correct Answer: (1) $y < 3$. All points in the shaded region have their y coordinate less than 3 since they are all below the $y = 3$ line. Since the line is dotted, y cannot equal 3. *(Equations and Inequalities)*

---

45. If $2ax - 5x = 2$, then x is equivalent to

    (1) $\dfrac{2 + 5a}{2a}$

    (2) $\dfrac{1}{a - 5}$

    (3) $\dfrac{2}{2a - 5}$

    (4) $7 - 2a$

Correct Answer: (3) $\dfrac{2}{2a - 5}$. Factor out x on the left side: $x(2a - 5) = 2$. Divide both sides by $2a - 5$: $x = \dfrac{2}{2a - 5}$. *(Equations and Inequalities)*

46. Which coordinate point is in the solution set for the system of inequalities shown in the accompanying graph?

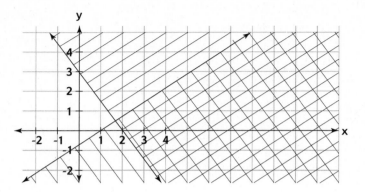

   (1) (3,1)
   (2) (2,2)
   (3) (1,–1)
   (4) (0,1)

Correct Answer: (1) (3,1). All the other choices are wrong because those points are not in the twice-shaded region. *(Equations and Inequalities)*

47. What is the value of x in the equation $\frac{x}{2} + \frac{x}{6} = 2$?
   (1) 12
   (2) 8
   (3) 3
   (4) $\frac{1}{4}$

Correct Answer: (3) 3. In order to cancel out the denominator of each fraction, multiply each piece by the common denominator of 6. This results in $3x + x = 12$. Combining like terms results in $4x = 12$. Dividing both sides by 4 gives you the solution of 3. *(Equations and Inequalities)*

48. In the accompanying diagram, a ladder leaning against a building makes an angle of 58° with level ground. If the distance from the foot of the ladder to the building is 6 feet, find, to the nearest foot, how far up the building the ladder will reach.

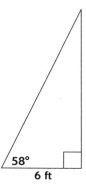

58°

6 ft

    (1) 9 feet

    (2) 10 feet

    (3) 20 feet

    (4) 12 feet

Correct Answer: (2) 10 feet. Since this is a right triangle, a trigometric ratio could be set up. Given is an angle and the adjacent side and the opposite side must be determined. Using $\tan 58° = \frac{x}{6\ ft}$, you find $x = 9.602$. Rounding this to the nearest foot would yield 10 feet. *(Trigometric Functions)*

49. Which ordered pair is *not* in the solution set of $y > 2x + 1$?

    (1) $(1, 4)$

    (2) $(1, 6)$

    (3) $(3, 8)$

    (4) $(2, 5)$

Correct Answer: (4) $(2, 5)$. Since a point is (x, y), the first coordinate is plugged in for x and the second for y. Plugging in $(2, 5)$ gives the inequality $5 > 2(2) + 1$. This simplifies to $5 > 5$, which is an untrue statement. *(Equations and Inequalities)*

50. What is the sum of $\frac{2}{x}$ and $\frac{x}{2}$?

  (1) 1

  (2) $\frac{2+x}{2x}$

  (3) $\frac{4+x}{2x}$

  (4) $\frac{4+x^2}{2x}$

Correct Answer: (4) $\frac{4+x^2}{2x}$. Sum means addition, so when you add $\frac{2}{x}$ and $\frac{x}{2}$, you find that the LCD is $2x$. $\left(\frac{2}{2}\right)\frac{2}{x} + \frac{x}{2}\left(\frac{x}{x}\right) = \frac{4}{2x} + \frac{x^2}{2x} = \frac{4+x^2}{2x}$. *(Variables and Expressions)*

51. If $x = 4$ and $y = -2$, the value of $\frac{1}{2}xy^2$ is

  (1) 32

  (2) 8

  (3) −4

  (4) −8

Correct Answer: (2) 8. $\frac{1}{2}xy^2 = \frac{1}{2}(4)(-2)^2 = \frac{1}{2}(4)(4) = \frac{1}{2}(16) = 8$. *(Variables and Expressions)*

52. Factored completely, the expression $2y^2 + 12y - 54$ is equivalent to

  (1) $2(y + 9)(y - 3)$

  (2) $2(y - 3)(y - 9)$

  (3) $(y + 6)(2y - 9)$

  (4) $(2y + 6)(y - 9)$

Correct Answer: (1) $2(y + 9)(y - 3)$. Factor out the 2: $2(y^2 + 6y - 27)$. Factor the trinomial: $2(y + 9)(y - 3)$. *(Variables and Expressions)*

53. The expression $(50x^3 - 60x^2 + 10x) \div 10x$ is equivalent to

(1) $5x^2 - 6x + 1$
(2) $5x^3 - 6x^2 + x$
(3) $5x^2 - 60x^2 + 10x$
(4) $5x^2 - 6x$

Correct Answer: (1) $5x^2 - 6x + 1$. Each piece of the trinomial must be divided by $10x$. Recall that when dividing, you subtract the exponents.

$50x^3 \div 10x = 5x^2$

$-60x^2 \div 10x = -6x$

$10x \div 10x = 1$

This makes your final answer choice (1) $5x^2 - 6x + 1$. *(Variables and Expressions)*

54. The inequality $\frac{1}{2}x + 3 < 2x - 6$ is equivalent to

(1) $x < -\frac{5}{6}$
(2) $x > -\frac{5}{6}$
(3) $x < 6$
(4) $x > 6$

Correct Answer: (4) $x > 6$. Subtract $\frac{1}{2}x$ from both sides: $3 < 1.5x - 6$. Add 6 to boths sides: $9 < 1.5x$. Divide both sides by 1.5: $x > 6$. *(Equations and Inequalities)*

55. If $x = -4$ and $y = 3$, what is the value of $x - 3y^2$?

(1) -13
(2) -23
(3) -31
(4) -85

Correct Answer: (3) -31. $x - 3y^2 = (-4) - 3(3)^2 = -4 - 27 = -31$. *(Variables and Expressions)*

56. Which expression represents the number of yards in x feet?

(1) $\frac{x}{12}$

(2) $\frac{x}{3}$

(3) $3x$

(4) $12x$

Correct Answer: (2) $\frac{x}{3}$. Let y = the number of yards. You know that 1 yard = 3 feet $\rightarrow \frac{y}{1} = \frac{x}{3} \rightarrow$ $y = \frac{x}{3}$. *(Equations and Inequalities)*

57. The expression $\frac{5x}{6} + \frac{x}{4}$ is equivalent to

(1) $\frac{3x}{5}$

(2) $\frac{5x^2}{10}$

(3) $\frac{13x}{12}$

(4) $\frac{5x}{24}$

Correct Answer: (3) $\frac{13x}{12}$. The LCD is 12. Multiply the numerator and denominator of the first fraction by 2 and the numerator and denominator of the second fraction by 3. $\frac{(2)5x}{(2)6} + \frac{x(3)}{4(3)}$. Combine the numerators while leaving the denominators unchanged: $\frac{13x}{12}$. *(Variables and Expressions)*

58. Mario paid $44.25 in taxi fare from the hotel to the airport. The cab charged $2.25 for the first mile plus $3.50 for each additional mile. How many miles was it from the hotel to the airport?

(1) 10

(2) 11

(3) 12

(4) 13

Correct Answer: (4) 13. You can use this information to set up the equation $C = 3.50m + 2.25$, where C is the total cost and m is the number of *additional* miles. You plug in Mario's taxi fare of $44.25 for C and solve for m. Subtracting 2.25 from each side gives you $42 = 3.50m$. Dividing both sides by 3.50 results in $m = 12$. You then add one to this amount to figure in the first mile of the trip. This gives you choice (4) 13. *(Patterns, Relations, and Functions)*

59. The graph of the equation $x + 3y = 6$ intersects the y-axis at the point whose coordinates are

  (1) $(0,2)$
  (2) $(0,6)$
  (3) $(0,18)$
  (4) $(6,0)$

Correct Answer: (1) $(0,2)$. When the graph of an equation intersects the y-axis, the x-coordinate is 0. Substituting $x = 0$ into the equation, you have $0 + 3y = 6 \rightarrow 3y = 6 \rightarrow y = 2$. *(Equations and Inequalities)*

60. If $2x^2 - x + 6$ is subtracted from $x^2 - 3x - 2$, the result is

  (1) $x^2 + 2x - 8$
  (2) $x^2 - 4x + 8$
  (3) $-x^2 + 2x - 8$
  (4) $-x^2 + 4x - 8$

Correct Answer: (4) $-x^2 + 4x - 8$. $2x^2 - x + 6$ is subtracted from $x^2 + 3x - 2 \rightarrow x^2 + 3x - 2 - (2x^2 - x + 6)$. Distribute the negative sign: $x^2 + 3x - 2 - 2x^2 + x - 6$. Combine like terms: $-x^2 + 4x - 8$. *(Variables and Expressions)*

61. The solution set for the equation $x^2 - 5x = 6$ is

  (1) $\{1, -6\}$
  (2) $\{2, -3\}$
  (3) $\{-1, 6\}$
  (4) $\{-2, 3\}$

Correct Answer: (3) $\{-1, 6\}$. First, set the equation equal to 0 by subtracting 6 from both sides to get $x^2 - 5x - 6 = 0$. Next factor the equation (what multiplies to -6 and adds to -5). The factors are $(x - 6)(x + 1)$. Set these equal to 0 and solve for x to get $x = -1$ and 6. *(Equations and Inequalities)*

62. The expression $(a^2 + b^2)^2$ is equivalent to

  (1) $a^2 + b^2$
  (2) $a^4 + a^2b^2 + b^4$
  (3) $a^4 + 2a^2b^2 + b^4$
  (4) $a^4 + 4a^2b^2 + b^4$

Correct Answer: (3) $a^4 + 2a^2b^2 + b^4$. $(a^2 + b^2)^2 = (a^2 + b^2)(a^2 + b^2) = a^4 + a^2b^2 + a^2b^2 + b^4$ $= a^4 + 2a^2b^2 + b^4$. *(Variables and Expressions)*

63. What is the solution set of the equation $x^2 - 5x = 0$?

(1) {0,–5}
(2) {0,5}
(3) {0}
(4) {5}

Correct Answer: (2) {0,5}. This is a quadratic equation that requires finding the greatest common factor: $x(x - 5) = 0$. Set each factor equal to 0 and solve: $x = 0$ and $x - 5 = 0$. This results in choice (2) with solutions 0 and 5. *(Equations and Inequalities)*

64. What is the value of w in the equation $\frac{3}{4}w + 8 = \frac{1}{3}w - 7$?

(1) 2.4
(2) –0.2
(3) –13.846
(4) –36

Correct Answer: (4) –36. Add 7 to both sides: $\frac{3}{8}w + 15 = \frac{1}{3}w$. Subtract $\frac{3}{4}w$ from both sides: $15 = -\frac{5}{12}w$. Multiply both sides by $\frac{12}{5}$: –36 = w. If you work backward from the answers by substituting each answer into the equation until you find the one that makes the equation true, you can determine that Choice (4) must be the correct one since the others do not work.

Incorrect Choices: $\frac{3}{4}(2.4) + 8 \overset{?}{=} \frac{1}{3}(2.4) - 7 \rightarrow 9.8 \neq 6.2$. Choice (1) doesn't work.

$\frac{3}{4}(-0.2) + 8 \overset{?}{=} \frac{1}{3}(-0.2) - 7 \rightarrow 7.85 \neq 7.0\overline{6}$. Choice (2) doesn't work.

$\frac{3}{4}(-13.846) + 8 \overset{?}{=} \frac{1}{3}(-13.846) - 7 \rightarrow -2.3845 \neq 11.6153$. Choice (3) doesn't work. *(Equations and Inequalities)*

65. Which inequality is represented in the accompanying graph?

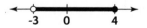

-3   0   4

(1) $-3 \leq x < 4$
(2) $-3 \leq x \leq 4$
(3) $-3 < x < 4$
(4) $-3 < x \leq 4$

Correct Answer: (4) $-3 < x \leq 4$. The shaded part of the line contains all numbers greater than but not equal to –3 and less than or equal to 4. *(Equations and Inequalities)*

---

66. One of the roots of the equation $x^2 + 3x - 18 = 0$ is 3. What is the other root?

    (1) 15
    (2) 6
    (3) −6
    (4) −21

Correct Answer: (3) −6. When you try all the choices to see which one works, you discover that when substituting $x = -6$: $(-6)^2 + 3(-6) - 18 = 0$, choice (3) works.

Incorrect Choices: Substitute $x = 15$: $(15)^2 + 3(15) - 18 = 252 \neq 0$. Choice (1) does not work.

Substitute $x = 6$: $(6)^2 + 3(6) - 18 = 36 \neq 0$. Choice (2) does not work.

Substitute $x = -21$: $(-21)^2 + 3(-21) - 18 \neq 0$. Choice (4) does not work. *(Equations and Inequalities)*

---

67. The expression $\dfrac{5x^6 y^2}{x^8 y}$ is equivalent to

    (1) $5x^2 y$
    (2) $\dfrac{5y}{x^2}$
    (3) $5x^{14} y^3$
    (4) $\dfrac{5y^3}{x^{14}}$

Correct Answer: (2) $\dfrac{5y}{x^2}$. When dividing monomials, divide or reduce the coefficients, look at the bases, and cancel an equal number of bases in the numerator and denominator, $\dfrac{x^6}{x^8} = \dfrac{xxxxxx}{xxxxxxxx}$. Therefore, all 6 x's in the numerator cancel with 6 x's in the denominator and x^2 is left in the denominator. Follow the same procedure for the y's, and a y will be left in the numerator. *(Variables and Expressions)*

---

68. The expression $(6x^3y^6)^2$ is equivalent to

    (1) $36x^6y^{12}$
    (2) $36x^5y^8$
    (3) $12x^6y^{12}$
    (4) $6x^6y^{12}$

Correct Answer: (1) $36x^6y^{12}$. You must raise each piece of the monomial to the second power. Recall that when you raise a power to another power, you must multiply the two powers.

$6^2 = 36$

$(x^3)^2 = x^6$

$(y^6)^2 = y^{12}$

This makes your final answer choice (1) $36x^6y^{12}$. *(Variables and Expressions)*

69. The expression $2x^2 - x^2$ is equivalent to

    (1) x^0

    (2) 2

    (3) x^2

    (4) $-2x^4$

Correct Answer: (3) x^2. When combining like terms, the variable stays the same; just combine the coefficients. Similarly, you can factor $x^2(2-1) = x^2(1) = x^2$. *(Variables and Expressions)*

70. The ratio of Tariq's telephone bill to Pria's telephone bill was 7:5. Tariq's bill was $14 more than Pria's bill. What was Tariq's bill?

    (1) $21

    (2) $28

    (3) $35

    (4) $49

Correct Answer: (4) $49. Let $7x$ = Tariq's telephone bill and let $5x$ = Pria's telephone bill. Then, $7x = 5x + 14$. Subtract 5x from both sides: $2x = 14$. Divide both sides by 2: $x = 7$. Tariq's telephone bill: $7x = 7(7) = 49$. *(Equations and Inequalities)*

71. When Albert flips open his mathematics textbook, he notices that the product of the page numbers of the two facing pages that he sees is 156. Which equation could be used to find the page numbers that Albert is looking at?

    (1) $x + (x + 1) = 156$

    (2) $(x + 1) + (x + 2) = 156$

    (3) $(x + 1)(x + 3) = 156$

    (4) $x(x + 1) = 156$

Correct Answer: (4) $x(x + 1) = 156$. If the pages face each other, the difference between the page numbers is one—or one page number is one more than the other. Let x = one page number; let $x + 1$ = the next page number. The product of these pages equals 156, which translates into $x(x + 1) = 156$. *(Equations and Inequalities)*

72. Which ratio represents cos A in the accompanying diagram of $\triangle ABC$?

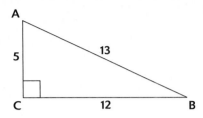

(1) $\frac{5}{13}$

(2) $\frac{12}{13}$

(3) $\frac{12}{5}$

(4) $\frac{13}{5}$

Correct Answer: (1) $\frac{5}{13}$. cos $A = \dfrac{adjacent\ side}{hypotenuse} = \frac{5}{13}$. *(Trigonometric Functions)*

73. Point $(k, -3)$ lies on the line whose equation is $x - 2y = -2$. What is the value of k?

(1) -8

(2) -6

(3) 6

(4) 8

Correct Answer: (1) -8. Substitute x with k and y with -3 into the equation. $x - 2y = -2 \rightarrow k - 2(-3) = -2 \rightarrow k + 6 = -2 \rightarrow k = -8$. *(Equations and Inequalities)*

74. If $(x - 4)$ is a factor of $x^2 - x - w = 0$, then the value of w is

(1) 12

(2) -12

(3) 3

(4) -3

Correct Answer: (1) 12. If $(x - 4)$ is a factor of $x^2 - x - w = 0$, then $x = 4$ is a root of the equation, so $4^2 - 4 - w = 0 \rightarrow 12 - w = 0 \rightarrow w = 12$. *(Equations and Inequalities)*

75. If $\frac{x}{4} - \frac{a}{b} = 0$, $b \neq 0$, then x is equal to

(1) $-\frac{a}{4b}$

(2) $\frac{a}{4b}$

(3) $-\frac{4a}{b}$

(4) $\frac{4a}{b}$

Correct Answer: (4) $\frac{4a}{b}$. First, add $\frac{a}{b}$ to both sides to get $\frac{x}{4} = \frac{a}{b}$. Solve this proportion by cross multiplying and getting x alone on one side: $4a = bx$. When you divide by b, then $x = \frac{4a}{b}$. *(Equations and Inequalities)*

76. The line $3x - 2y = 12$ has

(1) a slope of $\frac{3}{2}$ and a y-intercept of -6

(2) a slope of $-\frac{3}{2}$ and a y-intercept of 6

(3) a slope of 3 and a y-intercept of -2

(4) a slope of -3 and a y-intercept of -6

Correct Answer: (1) a slope of $\frac{3}{2}$ and a y-intercept of -6. The slope-y intercept form of a line's equation is $y = mx + b$, where m is its slope and y is its y-intercept.

Subtract $3x$ from both sides of the equation: $-2y = 12 - 3x$. Divide each term by -2: $y = -6 + \frac{3}{2}x = \frac{3}{2}x - 6$. Slope is $\frac{3}{2}$, and y-intercept is -6. *(Equations and Inequalities)*

77. Which line is perpendicular to the line whose equation is $5y + 6 = -3x$?

(1) $y = -\frac{5}{3}x + 7$

(2) $y = \frac{5}{3}x + 7$

(3) $y = -\frac{3}{5}x + 7$

(4) $y = \frac{3}{5}x + 7$

Correct Answer: (2) $y = \frac{5}{3}x + 7$. Two perpendicular lines have slopes that are negative reciprocals of each other. To find the slope of the given equation, you need to write it in $y = mx + b$ form. To isolate y: $5y + 6 = -3x$. Subtract 6 from both sides: $5y = -3x - 6$. Divide both sides by 5: $y = \frac{-3}{5}x - \frac{6}{5} \rightarrow m = \frac{-3}{5}$. A line perpendicular to the given line has slope $\frac{5}{3}$. *(Equations and Inequalities)*

78. If $3x$ is one factor of $3x^2 - 9x$, what is the other factor?

(1) $3x$
(2) $x^2 - 6x$
(3) $x - 3$
(4) $x + 3$

Correct Answer: (3) $x - 3$. $3x^2 - 9x = 3x(x - 3)$. *(Variables and Expressions)*

79. A rocket car on the Bonneville Salt Flats is traveling at a rate of 640 miles per hour. How much time would it take for the car to travel 384 miles at this rate?

(1) 36 minutes
(2) 245 minutes
(3) 256 minutes
(4) 1.7 hours

Correct Answer: (1) 36 minutes. Let d = distance, r = rate, and t = time. Then, $t = \frac{d}{r} = \frac{384}{640} = 0.6$ hours $= .6(60) = 36$ minutes. *(Equations and Inequalities)*

80. The number of people on the school board is represented by x. Two subcommittees with an equal number of members are formed, one with $\frac{2}{3}x - 5$ members and the other with $\frac{x}{4}$ members. How many people are on the school board?

(1) 20
(2) 12
(3) 8
(4) 4

Correct Answer: (2) 12. Since the subcommittees have the same number of members, set the expressions equal to each other:

$\frac{2}{3}x - 5 = \frac{x}{4}$. Multiply every term by 12, the lowest common denominator: $8x - 60 = 3x$.

Subtract $8x$ from both sides: $-60 = -5x$. Divide both sides by -5: $x = 12$. *(Equations and Inequalities)*

81. The accompanying diagram shows a kite has been secured to a stake in the ground with a 20-foot string. The kites is located 12 feet from the ground, directly over point *X*. What is the distance, in feet, between the stake and point *X*?

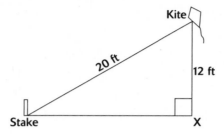

(1) 16 feet

(2) 14 feet

(3) 20 feet

(4) 24 feet

Correct Answer: (1) 16 feet. Use the Pythagorean Theorem to get $12^2 + b^2 = 20^2$. $144 + b^2 = 400$. $b^2 = 256$ and $b = 16$ feet. *(Trigonometric Functions)*

82. What is the least common denominator of $\frac{1}{2}, \frac{2}{7x}$, and $\frac{5}{x}$?

(1) $9x$

(2) $2x$

(3) $14x$

(4) $14x^2$

Correct Answer: (3) $14x$. The least common denominator is the smallest expression into which each denominator can be divided resulting in a whole number. *(Variables and Expressions)*

83. If the value of dependent variable *y* increases as the value of independent variable *x* increases, the graph of this relationship could be a

(1) horizontal line

(2) vertical line

(3) line with a negative slope

(4) line with a positive slope

Correct Answer: (4) line with a positive slope. If both *x* and *y* increase, then the change in *y* and the change in *x* have the same sign. This implies that the sign of $m = \frac{\Delta y}{\Delta x}$ is positive. *(Patterns, Relations, and Functions)*

84. Tara buys two items that cost d dollars each. She gives the cashier $20. Which expression represents the change she should receive?

(1) $20 - 2d$

(2) $20 - d$

(3) $20 + 2d$

(4) $2d - 20$

Correct Answer: (1) $20 - 2d$. From the $20, the cashier needs d for one item and another d for the other item, totaling $2d$. *(Variables and Expressions)*

85. Which linear equation represents the data in the accompanying table?

c	d
0	20.00
1	21.50
2	23.00
3	24.50

(1) $d = 1.50c$

(2) $d = 1.50c + 20.00$

(3) $d = 20.00c + 1.50$

(4) $d = 21.50c$

Correct Answer: (2) $d = 1.50c + 20.00$. The equation in choice (2) is the only one satisfying $c = 0$, $d = 20$. *(Equations and Inequalities)*

86. If the temperature in Buffalo is $23°$ Fahrenheit, what is the temperature in degrees Celsius? (Use the formula $C = \frac{5}{9}(F - 32)$.)

(1) -5

(2) 5

(3) -45

(4) 45

Correct Answer: (1) -5. $C = \frac{5}{9}(F - 32) = \frac{5}{9}(23 - 32) = \frac{5}{9}(-9) = -5$. *(Equations and Inequalities)*

87. For which value of x is the expression $\frac{x-7}{x+2}$ undefined?

(1) -2

(2) 2

(3) 7

(4) 0

Correct Answer: (1) -2. A fraction is undefined when its denominator is zero. $x + 2 = 0 \rightarrow x = -2$. *(Variables and Expressions)*

88. Parking charges at Superior Parking Garage are $5.00 for the first hour and $1.50 for each additional 30 minutes. If Margo has $12.50, what is the maximum amount of time she will be able to park her car at the garage?

(1) $2\frac{1}{2}$ hours

(2) $3\frac{1}{2}$ hours

(3) 6 hours

(4) $6\frac{1}{2}$ hours

Correct Answer: (2) $3\frac{1}{2}$ hours. Let $x =$ the number of hours Margo's car will be in the garage. Then $12.50 = \$5 + \$1.50x$. Subtract 5 from both sides: $7.50 = 1.50x$. Divide both sides by 1.50: $x = 3.5$. *(Equations and Inequalities)*

89. The expression $(3x^2 + 2xy + 7) - (6x^2 - 4xy + 3)$ is equivalent to

(1) $-3x^2 - 2xy + 4$

(2) $3x^2 - 2xy + 4$

(3) $-3x^2 + 6xy + 4$

(4) $3x^2 - 6xy - 4$

Correct Answer: (3) $-3x^2 + 6xy + 4$. Distribute the negative sign: $3x^2 + 2xy + 7 - 6x^2 + 4xy - 3 = -3x^2 + 6xy + 4$. *(Variables and Expressions)*

90. If $3(x - 2) = 2x + 6$, the value of x is

(1) 0

(2) 5

(3) 12

(4) 20

Correct Answer: (3) 12. Distribute the 3 on the left side: $3x - 6 = 2x + 6$. Add 6 to both sides: $3x = 2x + 12$. Subtract $2x$ from both sides: $x = 12$. *(Equations and Inequalities)*

91. What point is the intersection of the graphs of the lines $2x - y = 3$ and $x + y = 3$?

(1) (2,1)

(2) (1,2)

(3) (3,0)

(4) (3,3)

Correct Answer: (1) (2,1). The intersection point of two graphs is the point they have in common. Work back from the answers: try choice (1), substitute $x = 2$ and $y = 1$ into both equations. Since both equations are satisfied, (2, 1) is the solution. *(Equations and Inequalities)*

Open-Ended Questions

92. Find all negative odd integers that satisfy the following inequality:

$-3x + 1 \leq 17$

Correct Answer: -5, -3, and -1. The first step is to subtract one from both sides and then divide both sides by -3. When you multiply or divide an inequality by a negative, you must switch the direction of the sign. This yields $x \geq -5\frac{1}{3}$. The negative odd integers that are greater than $-5\frac{1}{3}$ are -5, -3, and -1. *(Equations and Inequalities)*

93. Running at a constant speed, Andrea covers 15 miles in $2\frac{1}{2}$ hours. At this speed, how many *minutes* will it take her to run 2 miles?

Correct Answer: It will take Andrea 20 minutes to run 2 miles.

2.5 hours = 150 minutes; $\frac{15}{150} = \frac{2}{x}$. Cross-multiply: $15x = 300$. Divide both sides by 15: $x = 20$ minutes. *(Patterns, Relations, and Functions)*

94. Julio's wages vary directly as the number of hours that he works. If his wages for 5 hours are $29.75, how much will he earn for 30 hours?

Correct Answer: $178.50. Per hour, Julio makes $\frac{\$29.75}{5 \text{ hours}} = \$5.95/\text{hour}$. In 30 hours he'll earn $5.95(30) = $178.50. Alternately, $30 = 6 \times 5$, so $5 \times \$29.75 = \$178.50$. *(Patterns, Relations, and Functions)*

95. Every month, Omar buys pizzas to serve at a party for his friends. In May, he bought three more than twice the number of pizzas he bought in April. If Omar bought 15 pizzas in May, how many pizzas did he buy in April?

Correct Answer: 6. Let x = the number of pizzas bought in April. Then you can use $2x + 3$ to represent the number of pizzas bought in May. Therefore, $2x + 3 = 15$. Solve for x. *(Equation and Inequalities)*

96. Factor completely: $3ax^2 - 27a$

Correct Answer: $3a(x^2 - 9) = 3a(x - 3)(x + 3)$. *(Variables and Expressions)*

97. Solve for x: $3.3 - x = 3(x - 1.7)$

Correct Answer: 2.1. $3.3 - x = 3(x - 1.7) \rightarrow 3.3 - x = 3x - 5.1$. Add x and 5.1 to both sides: $8.4 = 4x \rightarrow 2.1 = x$; $x = 2.1$. *(Equations and Inequalities)*

98. The formula $C = \frac{5}{9}(F - 32)$ is used to convert Fahrenheit temperature, F, to Celsius temperature, C. What temperature, in degrees Fahrenheit, is equivalent to a temperature of 10° Celsius?

Correct Answer: 50°. Plug in 10 for C and solve for F. After multiplying both sides by (9/5) you get 18 = F − 32. Adding 32 to both sides results in an answer of 50°. *(Equations and Inequalities)*

99. Simplify: $\dfrac{x^2 + 6x + 5}{x^2 - 25}$

Correct Answer: $\dfrac{(x + 1)}{(x - 5)}$

$\dfrac{x^2 + 6x + 5}{x^2 - 25}$. Factor both denominator and numerator: $\dfrac{(x + 1)(x + 5)}{(x - 5)(x + 5)}$. Divide out $(x + 5)$: $\dfrac{(x + 1)}{(x - 5)}$.
(Variables and Inequalities)

100. Bob and Latoya both drove to a baseball game at a college stadium. Bob lives 70 miles from the stadium, and Latoya lives 60 miles from it, as shown in the accompanying diagram. Bob drove at a rate of 50 miles per hour, and Latoya drove at a rate of 40 miles per hour. If they both left home at the same time, who got to the stadium first?

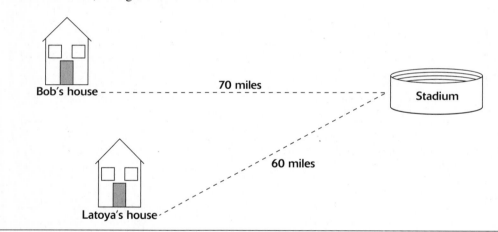

Correct Answer: Bob gets to the stadium first. To find the time it takes Bob and Latoya to drive to the stadium, use the formula time $= \dfrac{\text{distance}}{\text{rate}}$.

$\text{Time}_{Bob} = \dfrac{70}{50} = 1.4$ hours, $\text{Time}_{Latoya} = \dfrac{60}{40} = 1.5$ hours.

Since it takes Bob less time to get to the stadium, he gets there first. *(Patterns, Relations, and Functions)*

101. From a point on level ground 25 feet from the base of a tower, the angle of elevation to the top of the tower is 78°, as shown in the accompanying diagram. Find the height of the tower, to the *nearest tenth of a foot.*

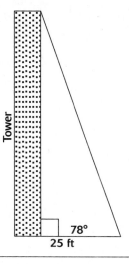

Correct Answer: 117.6. Since this is a right triangle and you are concerned with the sides opposite and adjacent to the 78° angle, you should use the tangent ratio: tan 78 = x/25. If you place tan 78 over 1 and multiply each side by 25, you get the rounded answer 117.6 feet. *(Trigonometric Functions)*

102. Write an irrational number and explain why it is irrational.

Correct Answer: An irrational number is a decimal number that never terminates and that has no pattern in its digits. Examples of irrational numbers: π, $\sqrt{2}$, $\sqrt{5}$, and so on. *(Number Systems)*

103. The accompanying diagram shows a flagpole that stands on level ground. Two cables, *r* and *s*, are attached to the pole at a point 16 feet above the ground. The combined length of the two cables is 50 feet. If cable *r* is attached to the ground 12 feet from the base of the pole, what is the measure of the angle, *x*, to the *nearest degree*, that cable *s* makes with the ground?

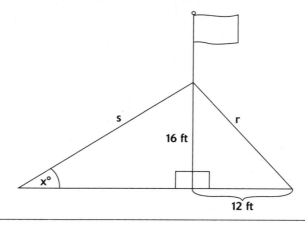

Correct Answer: $x = 32°$. First find *r* by using the Pythagorean Theorem ($12^2 + 16^2 = r^2$). You'll get that *r* equals 20 ft. Then it's given that *r* and *s* combined is 50 ft, so that means *s* equals 30 ft. Now use SOH CAH TOA to set up an equation to solve for *x*, ($\sin x° = \frac{16}{30}$). On the calculator, $\sin^{-1}(16/30) =$ 32.23095264, which rounded to the nearest degree becomes 32°. *(Trigonometric Functions)*

---

104. Tamara has two sisters. One of the sisters is 7 years older than Tamara. The other sister is 3 years younger than Tamara. The product of Tamara's sisters' ages is 24. How old is Tamara?

Correct Answer: Tamara is 5 years old. Let x = Tamara's age, $x + 7$ = Tamara's older sister's age, and $x - 3$ = Tamara's younger sister's age. $(x + 7)(x - 3) = 24$. Distribute the left side and subtract 24 from both sides: $x^2 + 4x - 45 = 0$. Factor: $(x + 9)(x - 5) = 0$. Set each factor equal to 0:

$x + 9 = 0 \rightarrow x = -9$

$x - 5 = 0 \rightarrow x = 5$

Reject –9 because age cannot be negative. *(Equations and Inequalities)*

---

105. Factor completely: $5n^2 - 80$

Correct Answer: $5(n - 4)(n + 4)$ First factor out the G.C.F. of 5 to get $5(n^2 - 16)$. Now factor $n^2 - 16$ to get $(n - 4)(n + 4)$. To write the answer write the G.C.F. and remaining factors next to each other, so $5(n - 4)(n + 4)$. *(Variables and Expressions)*

106. Graph the following systems of inequalities on the accompanying set of axes and label the solution set S:

$y > x - 4$

$y + x \geq 2$

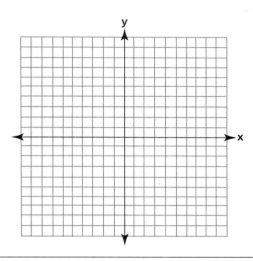

Correct Answer: Only a graphic solution can receive full credit. *(Equations and Inequalities)*

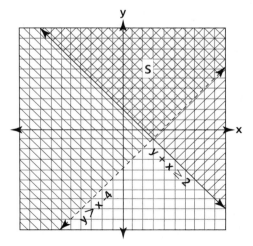

107. Factor completely: $3x^2 + 15x - 42$

Correct Answer: $3(x + 7)(x - 2)$. Factor completely usually indicates that there will be more than one step in factoring. Look for a greatest common factor among the terms, which is 3, so factor out a 3, and you're left with $x^2 + 5x - 14$ to factor. This factors into $(x + 7)(x - 2)$. Write the solution as the product of all the factors $3(x + 7)(x - 2)$. *(Variables and Expressions)*

108. A candy store sells 8-pound bags of mixed hazelnuts and cashews. If c pounds of cashews are in a bag, the price p of the bag can be found using the formula $p = 2.59c + 1.72(8 - c)$. If one bag is priced at \$18.11, how many pounds of cashews does it contain?

Correct Answer: $c = 5$. Substitute p with 18.11 and solve for c:

$18.11 = 2.59c + 1.72(8 - c)$. Distribute 1.72: $18.11 = 2.59c + 13.76 - 1.72c$.

Combine like terms: $18.11 = 13.76 + 0.87c$. Subtract 13.76 from both sides: $4.35 = 0.87c$. Divide both sides by 0.87: $5 = c$. *(Equations and Inequalities)*

109. Using only 32-cent and 20-cent stamps, Charlie put \$3.36 postage on a package he sent to his sister. He used twice as many 32-cent stamps as 20-cent stamps. Determine how many of *each* type of stamp he used.

Correct Answer: Charlie used eight 32-cent stamps and four 20-cent stamps.

Use trial and error, keeping in mind that Charlie bought twice as many 32-cent stamps as 20-cent stamps:

Number of 20-cent stamps	Number of 32-cent stamps	Total Spent
1	2	1(20) + 2(32) = \$0.84
2	4	2(20) + 4(32) = \$1.68
3	6	3(20) + 6(32) = \$2.52
4	8	4(20) + 8(32) = \$3.36

(Patterns, Relations, and Functions)

110. Sharu has \$2.35 in nickels and dimes. If he has a total of thirty-two coins, how many of *each* coin does he have?

Correct Answer: Sharu has 17 nickels and 15 dimes. Let x = the number of nickels, y = the number of dimes. Then $5x$ = total number of cents made up of nickels. $10y$ = total number of cents made up of dimes.

So, $x + y = 32$. Multiple the first equation by -10: $-10x - 10y = -320$.

Add the equations to eliminate x: $5x + 10y = 235$; $\quad 5x + 10y = 235$; $\quad -5x = -85$.

Divide both sides by -5: $x = 17$ nickels. Since $x + y = 32$, $y = 15$ dimes. *(Equations and Inequalities)*

111. Solve for x: $\frac{1}{16}x + \frac{1}{4} = \frac{1}{2}$.

Correct Answer: $x = 4$. Multiply each term by the lowest common denominator, 16, and simplify. $(16)\frac{1}{16}x + (16)\frac{1}{4} = (16)\frac{1}{2}$. Each 16 divides out each denominator: $x + 4 = 8$. Subtract 4 from both sides: $x = 4$. *(Equations and Inequalities)*

112. In a survey of 400 teenage shoppers at a large mall, 240 said they shopped at Abernathy's, 210 said they shopped at Bongo Republic, and 90 said they shopped at both stores. How many of the teenage shoppers surveyed did not shop at either store?

Correct Answer: 40 did not shop at either store. Draw a Venn Diagram of 2 circles overlapping each other. Let the one circle represent those who shop at Abernathy's and the other circle those who shop at Bongo Republic. The overlapping area represents those who shop at both. Put 90 in the overlapping area, 150 (240 – 90) in the nonoverlapping part of the Abernathy circle and 120(210 – 90) in the nonoverlapping part of the Bongo Republic circle. Add these (90 + 150 + 120) and subtract from 400 to get 40. An alternate algebraic solution would be to add 240 and 210 together and subtract out 90 to get 360. Subtract 360 from 400 to get 40. *(Patterns, Relations, and Functions)*

113. Walter is a waiter at the Towne Diner. He earns a daily wage of \$50, plus tips that are equal to 15% of the total cost of the dinners he serves. What was the total cost of the dinners he served if he earned \$170 on Tuesday?

Correct Answer: \$800. Let x = the total cost of the dinners Walter serves. Then $50 + .15x = 170$. Subtract 50 from both sides: $.15x = 120$. Divide both sides by $.15$: $x = 800$. *(Equations and Inequalities)*

114. Solve for x: $x^2 + 2x - 24 = 0$

Correct Answer: $x = -6$, $x = 4$

$x^2 + 2x - 24 = 0$. Factor: $(x + 6)(x - 4) = 0$. Set each factor equal to 10:

$x + 6 = 0$

$x - 4 = 0$

Subtract 0 from both sides of the first factor: $x = -6$. Add 4 to both sides of the second factor: $x = 4$. *(Equations and Inequalities)*

115. A person measures the angle of depression from the top of a wall to a point on the ground. The point is located on level ground 62 feet from the base of the wall, and the angle of depression is 52°. How high is the wall, to the *nearest tenth of a foot*?

Correct Answer: The wall is 79.4 ft. high.

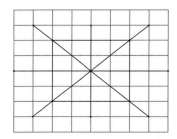

Tan $52° = \frac{x}{62} \rightarrow 62(\tan 52°) = x \rightarrow x = 79.4$ ft. *(Trigonometric Functions)*

116. In the accompanying diagram, the base of a 15-foot ladder rests on the ground 4 feet from a 6 foot fence.

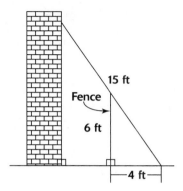

a. If the ladder touches the top of the fence and the side of a building, what angle, to the *nearest degree*, does the ladder make with the ground?

b. Using the angle found in part *a*, determine how far the top of the ladder reaches up the side of the building, to the *nearest foot*.

Correct Answer: *a.* The ladder makes an angle of 56° with the ground.

Label the larger triangle *ABC*. The angle the ladder makes with the ground is angle *A*.

$\tan A = \dfrac{6}{4} \rightarrow A = \tan^{-1}\left(\dfrac{6}{4}\right) = 56.309° \approx 56°$.

b. The top of the ladder reaches 12 feet up the side of the building.

To find the length of $BC \rightarrow \sin A = \dfrac{BC}{BA} \rightarrow \sin 56° = \dfrac{BC}{15}$. Multiple both sides by 15: $15\sin 56° = BC \rightarrow BC = 12.436$ feet ≈ 12 feet. *(Trigonometric Functions)*

117. The manufacturer of Ron's car recommends that the tire pressure be at least 26 pounds per square inch and less than 35 pounds per square inch. On the accompanying number line, graph the inequality that represents the recommended tire pressure.

Correct Answer: Label the number line so that the numbers from 26 to 35 are included. Put a filled-in circle above the 26 on the number line and an open circle above the 35 on the number line and draw a line from the one circle to the other. Ron's tire pressure can be any number greater than or equal to 26 pounds per square inch but can't be 35 pounds per square inch or go over 35 pounds per square inch. The inequality to represent this is $26 \leq n < 35$. *(Equations and Inequalities)*

118. A tree casts a shadow that is 20 feet long. The angle of elevation from the end of the shadow to the top of the tree is 66°. Determine the height of the tree, to the *nearest foot.*

Correct Answer: 45 feet. Draw a right triangle to model this situation. The shadow is the base of the right triangle, which is 20 feet. The angle of elevation is the angle between the base and hypotenuse of the right triangle. This problem involves SOH CAH TOA. You need to find the height, which is the other leg of the triangle. Tangent is the trigonometric function that does not involve the hypotenuse. Set up the equation $\tan 66° = \frac{h}{20}$. Solve this by multiplying 20 by tan 66° to get 44.921 feet, which rounds to 45 feet. *(Trigonometric Functions)*

119. Solve for all values of x that satisfy the equation $\frac{x}{x+3} = \frac{5}{x+7}$.

Correct Answer: $x = -5 \lor x = 3$; $\frac{x}{x+3} = \frac{5}{x+7}$. Cross-multiply: $x^2 + 7x = 5x + 15$. Subtract $5x$ and 15 from both sides: $x^2 + 2x - 15 = 0$. Factor: $(x + 5)(x - 3) = 0$. Set each factor equal to zero: $(x + 5) = 0. \lor (x - 3) = 0$. Solve for x: $x = -5 \lor x = 3$. *(Equations and Inequalities)*

120. Brett was given the problem: "Evaluate $2x^2 + 5$ when $x = 3$." Brett wrote that the answer was 41. Was Brett correct? Explain your answer.

Correct Answer: No, Brett was not correct. When $x = 3$, $2x^2 + 5 = 2(3)^2 + 5 = 2(9) + 5 = 23$. *(Variables and Expressions)*

121. Solve the following system of equations:

$$y = x^2 + 4x + 1$$

$$y = 5x + 3$$

(The use of the grid is optional.)

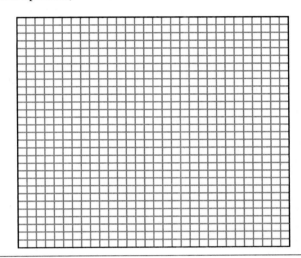

Correct Answer: $(-1, -2)$ and $(2, 13)$. To solve algebraically, solving a system means to find where the two equations are equal or intersect. Set one equation equal to the other to get $x^2 + 4x + 1 = 5x + 3$. Get one side equal to zero to get $x^2 - x - 2 = 0$.* Factor this into $(x - 2)(x + 1) = 0$. Set each factor equal to 0 and solve for x. The x-coordinates are w$x = -1$ and $x = 2$. Plug these values into one of the preceding equations to get the corresponding y-values ($y = 5(-1)+3$ and $y = 5(2) +3$). When $x = -1$, $y = -2$ and when $x = 2$, $y = 13$. Check these to make sure they work in the other equation.

The alternate solution would be to graph both equations and find the points of intersection. *(Equations and Inequalities)*

122. A ribbon 56 centimeters long is cut into two pieces. One of the pieces is three times longer than the other. Find the length, in centimeters, of both pieces of ribbon.

Correct Answer: Longer piece = 42 cm, and shorter piece = 14 cm. First pick a variable to represent the shorter piece of ribbon, such as n. The longer piece is 3 times longer than the shorter, so it must be $3n$. Set up an equation $n + 3n = 56$, which then becomes $4n = 56$, and $n = 14$. 14 cm is the shorter piece and 3 times 14 is 42 cm, which is the longer piece. *(Equations and Inequalities)*

123. The tickets for a dance recital cost $5.00 for adults and $2.00 for children. If the total number of tickets sold was 295 and the total amount collected was $1,220, how many adult tickets were sold? (Only an algebraic solution can receive full credit.)

Correct Answer: 210 adults. This is a system of equations problem and cannot be solved by trial and error for full credit. The first equation is $x + y = 295$, where x is the number of adults and y is the number of children. The second equation is $5x + 2y = 1220$. Solving the first equation for y yields $y = 295 - x$. Plugging that into the second equation gives $5x + 2(295 - x) = 1220$. When solved, $x = 210$. This is the number of adults. *(Equations and Inequalities)*

Geometry

Multiple-Choice Questions

1. Which diagram shows a dotted line that is *not* a line of symmetry?

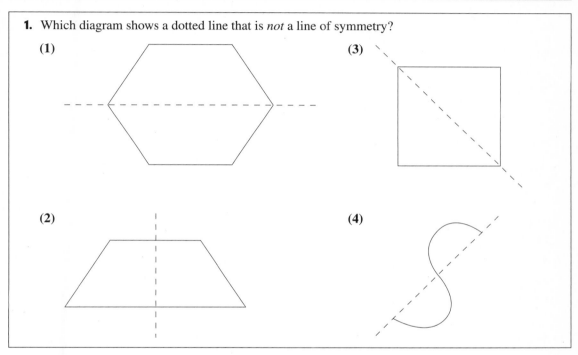

(1)

(2)

(3)

(4)

Correct Answer: (4)

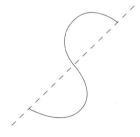

The dotted line crossing the letter S is not a line of symmetry because when the letter is reflected along this line, the points on one side of the line do not coincide with the points on the other side of the line. *(Transformations)*

2. A picture held by a magnet to a refrigerator slides to the bottom of the refrigerator, as shown in the accompanying diagram.

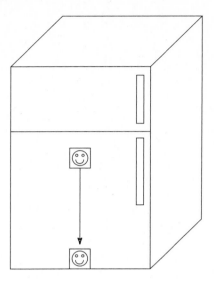

The change of position is an example of a

(1) translation
(2) dilation
(3) rotation
(4) reflection

Correct Answer: (1) translation. A translation indicates that an object has been moved or "slid" to another location. The magnet slid down the refrigerator to another place. *(Transformational Geometry)*

3. In the accompanying diagram, line *a* intersects line *b*.

What is the value of *x*?

(1) −10

(2) 5

(3) 10

(4) 90

Correct Answer: (3) 10. Since vertical angles are equal, $2x - 5 = x + 5$. Subtract *x* from both sides: $x - 5 = 5$. Add 5 to both sides: $x = 10$. *(Geometric Relationships)*

4. Which image represents a line reflection?

(1) Ρ ٩

(2) Ρ
     ௳

(3) Ρ
     Ρ

(4) Ρ
     Ρ

Correct Answer: (1)

Ρ ٩

A reflection transforms a figure over a fixed line so that each point has an image over the line. The line of reflection is also a line of symmetry between the original figure and its image. Choice (2) represents a rotation; choice (3) represents a translation; and choice (4) represents a dilation. *(Transformational Geometry)*

5. The perimeter of $\triangle A'B'C'$, the image of $\triangle ABC$, is twice as large as the perimeter of $\triangle ABC$. Which type of transformation has taken place?

(1) dilation
(2) translation
(3) rotation
(4) reflection

Correct Answer: (1) dilation. Choices 2, 3, and 4 all maintain the size of the original triangle. Choice 1 is the only transformation that changes the size of the original triangle. *(Transformational Geometry)*

6. What is the image of (x,y) after a translation of 3 units right and 7 units down?

(1) $(x + 3, y - 7)$
(2) $(x + 3, y + 7)$
(3) $(x - 3, y - 7)$
(4) $(x - 3, y + 7)$

Correct Answer: (1) $(x + 3, y - 7)$. Moving a point to the right 3 units means 3 is added to x; moving a point 7 units down means subtracting 7 from y. *(Transformational Geometry)*

7. Tina wants to sew a piece of fabric into a scarf in the shape of an isosceles triangle, as shown in the accompanying diagram.

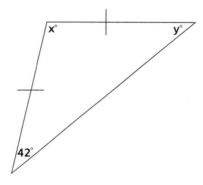

What are the values of x and y?

(1) $x = 42$ and $y = 96$
(2) $x = 69$ and $y = 69$
(3) $x = 90$ and $y = 48$
(4) $x = 96$ and $y = 42$

Correct Answer: (4) $x = 96$ and $y = 42$. All angles in a triangle add up to 180°, and since this is an isosceles triangle, the two angles across from the equal sides are equal, so $y = 42$. $180 - (42 + 42) = 96$. *(Shapes)*

8. Mrs. Brewer's art class is drawing reflected images. She wants her students to draw images reflected in a line. Which diagram represents a correctly drawn image?

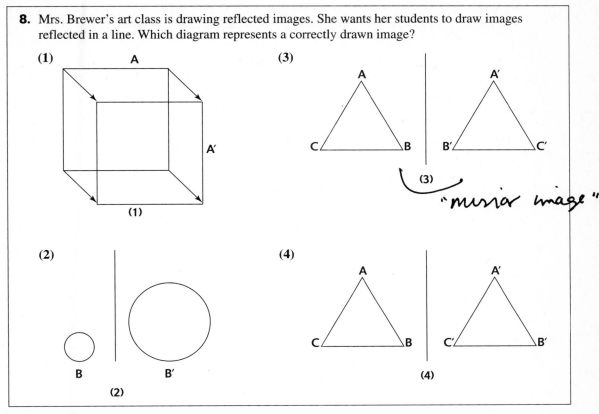

(1)

A

A′

(1)

(3)

A

A′

C   B   B′   C′

(3)

"mirror image"

(2)

B   B′

(2)

(4)

A

A′

C   B   C′   B′

(4)

Correct Answer: (3)

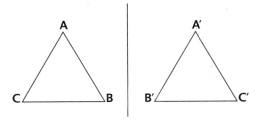

A   A′

C   B   B′   C′

When a point is reflected in a line its image is the same distance from the line as the original point. The object image is the same size and shape as the original object. *(Transformational Geometry)*

9. The NuFone Communications Company must run a telephone line between two poles at opposite ends of a lake, as shown in the accompanying diagram. The length and the width of the lake are 75 feet and 30 feet, respectively.

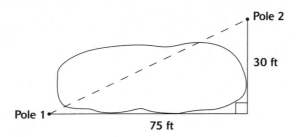

What is the distance between the two poles, to the nearest foot?

(1) 105

(2) 81

(3) 69

(4) 45

Correct Answer: (2) 81. Since it is a right triangle, the Pythagorean theorem can be used. $30^2 + 75^2 = c^2$, where c is the distance between the poles along the dotted line. It becomes $c = 80.77$, which rounded to the nearest foot is 81 feet. *(Geometric Relationships)*

10. Which set could *not* represent the lengths of the sides of a triangle?

(1) {3, 4, 5}

(2) {2, 5, 9}

(3) {5, 10, 12}

(4) {7, 9, 11}

Correct Answer: (2) {2, 5, 9}. The sum of the two smallest sides of a triangle has to be greater than the largest side. $2 + 5 = 7$, and 7 is not greater than 9 so {2, 5, 9} cannot represent the sides of a triangle. *(Geometric Relationships)*

11. The accompanying diagram shows two parallel roads, Hope Street and Grand Street, crossed by a transversal road, Broadway.

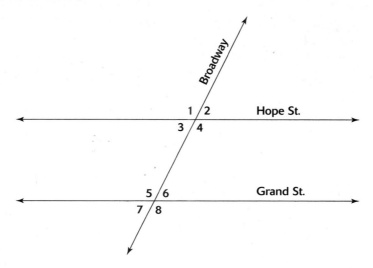

If $m\angle 1 = 110$, what is the measure of $\angle 7$?

(1) 40°
(2) 70°
(3) 110°
(4) 180°

Correct Answer: (2) 70°. The measures of $\angle 1$ and $\angle 5$ are equal because they are corresponding angles in this diagram. $\angle 5$ and $\angle 7$ are supplementary because they form a linear pair. Therefore, $m\angle 7 + 110 = 180$. Solving this equation results in 70 for $m\angle 7$. *(Geometric Relationships)*

12. One function of a movie projector is to enlarge the image on the film. This procedure is an example of a

(1) line of symmetry
(2) line reflection
(3) translation
(4) dilation

Correct Answer: (4) dilation. When a movie projector—or a Xerox machine—enlarges a picture, it does so proportionally. This is called a dilation. *(Transformational Geometry)*

13. The accompanying figure represents a section of bathroom tile ... ... shaped like regular hexagons.

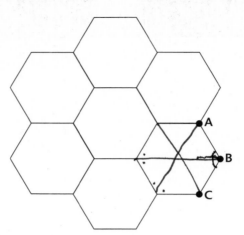

What is the measure of angle *ABC*?

(1) 60°
(2) 90°
(3) 120°
(4) 150°

Correct Answer: (3) 120°. To find the sum of all the interior angles of the hexagon, multiply 180° by (number of sides of hexagon – 2) to get 720°. Divide this by 6 (number of angles) to get 120°, the measure of each interior angle. *(Geometric Relationships)*

14. The image of point (3, –5) under the translation that shifts (x, y) to $(x – 1, y – 3)$ is

(1) (–4, 8)
(2) (–3, 15)
(3) (2, 8)
(4) (2, –8)

Correct Answer: (4) (2, –8). A translation is sliding a point. Plugging in 3 for x and –5 for y yields (3 – 1, –5 – 3), which is (2, –8). *(Transformational Geometry)*

15. In the accompanying diagram, parallel lines $\overleftrightarrow{AB}$ and $\overleftrightarrow{CD}$ are intersected by a transversal at points G and H, respectively, $m\angle AGH = x + 15$, and $m\angle GHD = 2x$.

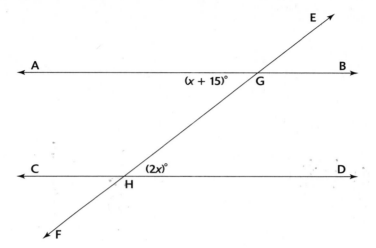

Which equation can be used to find the value of x?

(1) $2x = x + 15$
(2) $2x + x + 15 = 180$
(3) $2x + x + 15 = 90$
(4) $2x(x + 15) = 0$

Correct Answer: (1) $2x = x + 15$. When two parallel lines are cut by a transversal, the acute angles formed are congruent. Also, alternate interior angles are congruent. *(Geometric Relationships)*

16. The statement "If x is prime, then it is odd" is *false* when x equals

(1) 1
(2) 2
(3) 3
(4) 4

Correct Answer: (2) 2. This is a conditional statement, and conditional statements are false when the first part (hypothesis) is true and the second part (conclusion) is false. The number 2 makes "if x is prime" true; however, 2 is not true for "then it is odd." *(Informal Proof)*

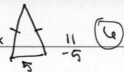

17. The base of an isosceles triangle is 5, and its perimeter is 11. The base of a similar isosceles triangle is 10. What is the perimeter of the larger triangle?

  (1) 15
  (2) 21
  (3) 22
  (4) 110

Correct Answer: (3) 22. Since the sides of similar triangles are in proportion, you can set up an equation such as $5/11 = 10/x$. Cross-multiplying gives you $110 = 5x$. Dividing each side by 5 results in the answer of 22. *(Shapes)*

18. Which letter has point symmetry but *not* line symmetry?

  (1) H
  (2) S
  (3) T
  (4) X

Correct Answer: (2) S. Point symmetry means the shape will look the same when spun around a point. Choice 1 and choice 4 have both point and line symmetry. Choice 3 has line symmetry, but not point symmetry. Choice 2 is only one with point symmetry but not line. *(Transformational Geometry)*

19. What is the converse of the statement "If it is Sunday, then I do not go to school"?

  (1) If I do not go to school, then it is Sunday.
  (2) If it is not Sunday, then I do not go to school.
  (3) If I go to school, then it is not Sunday.
  (4) If it is not Sunday, then I go to school.

Correct Answer: (1) If I do not go to school, then it is Sunday. The converse of a statement means to have the first part (hypothesis) and second part (conclusion) switch places. *(Informal Proofs)*

20. Which type of transformation is illustrated in the accompanying diagram?

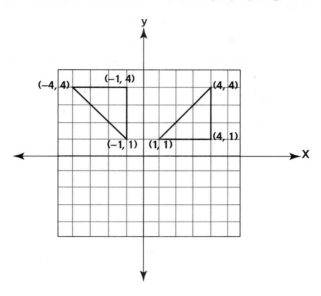

(1) dilation
(2) reflection
(3) translation
(4) rotation

Correct Answer: (4) rotation. If you rotate the right triangle counterclockwise, the second triangle will be constructed. *(Transformational Geometry)*

21. In the accompanying diagram, $\overleftrightarrow{AB} \parallel \overleftrightarrow{CD}$. From point E on $\overleftrightarrow{AB}$ transversals $\overrightarrow{EF}$ and $\overrightarrow{EG}$ are drawn, intersecting $\overrightarrow{CD}$ at H and I, respectively.

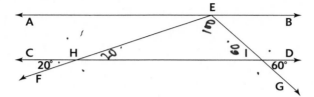

If $m\angle CHF = 20$ and $m\angle DIG = 60$, what is $m\angle HEI$?

(1) 60

(2) 80

(3) 100

(4) 120

Correct Answer: (3) 100. $\angle CHF$ and $\angle EHI$ are vertical angles so they are congruent; thus $m\angle EHI = 20°$. $\angle DIG$ and $\angle HIE$ are vertical angles so they are congruent; thus $\angle HIE = 60°$. Since $m\angle HIE + m\angle EHI = 80°$ and the sum of all angles in a triangle is $180°$, $m\angle HEI = 100°$. *(Geometric Relationships)*

22. Which graph represents the equation $x = 2$?

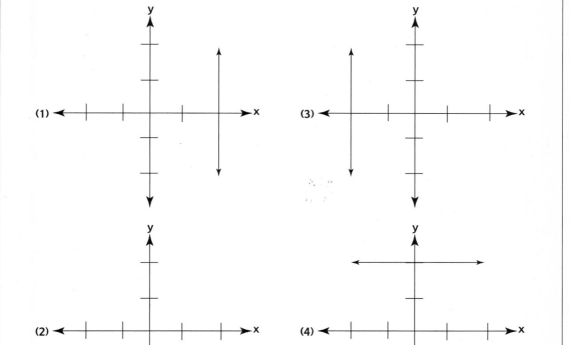

Correct Answer: (1) The equation of $x = c$ where c is a constant, is the graph of a vertical line that intersects the x-axis at c. (Coordinate Geometry)

23. The graph of the equation $x^2 + y^2 = r^2$ forms

(1) a circle
(2) a parabola
(3) a straight line
(4) two intersecting lines

Correct Answer: (1) a circle. This is the standard equation form of a circle. A circle's equation has x^2 and y^2 terms, while a parabola has only one squared term and a line has no squared terms. *(Shapes)*

24. What is the sum, in degrees, of the measures of the interior angles of a pentagon?

    (1) 180
    (2) 360
    (3) 540
    (4) 900

Correct Answer: (3) The formula to find the sum of the interior angles is $(n - 2) \times 180$, where n is the number of sides on the polygon. There are 5 sides on a pentagon, so $(5 - 2) \times 180 = 540$. *(Geometric Relations)*

25. Which quadrilateral must have diagonals that are congruent and perpendicular?

    (1) rhombus
    (2) square
    (3) trapezoid
    (4) parallelogram

Correct Answer: (2) One of the properties that a square has is that the diagonals are congruent and perpendicular. *(Shapes)*

26. The lengths of the sides of home plate on a baseball field are represented by the expressions in the accompanying figure.

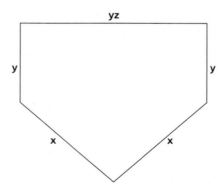

Which expression represents the perimeter of the figure?

    (1) $5xyz$
    (2) $x^2 + y^3z$
    (3) $2x + 3yz$
    (4) $2x + 2y + yz$

Correct Answer: (4) $2x + 2y + yz$. The perimeter of a figure is the sum of the lengths of all of its sides; in this case, $x + x + y + y + yz = 2x + 2y + yz$. *(Geometric Relationships)*

27. Jordan and Missy are standing together in the schoolyard. Jordan, who is 6 feet tall, casts a shadow that is 54 inches long. At the same time, Missy casts a shadow that is 45 inches long. How tall is Missy?

(1) 38 in
(2) 86.4 in
(3) 5 ft
(4) 5 ft 6 in

Correct Answer: (3) 5 ft. The children's shadows and their heights are proportional. Let x = Missy's height. Then, $\frac{6}{54} = \frac{x}{45}$. Cross-multiply: $6(45) = 54x \rightarrow 270 = 54x$. Divide both sides by 54: $x = 5$ feet. *(Geometric Relationships)*

28. The length of a side of a square window in Jessica's bedroom is represented by $2x - 1$. Which expression represents the area of the window?

(1) $2x^2 + 1$
(2) $4x^2 + 1$
(3) $4x^2 + 4x - 1$
(4) $4x^2 - 4x + 1$

Correct Answer: (4) Area of a square is side times side. Multiply $(2x - 1)(2x - 1)$. Use FOIL method or distributing to get choice 4. *(Shapes)*

29. Sean knows the length of the base, b, and the area, A, of a triangular window in his bedroom. Which formula could he use to find the height, h, of this window?

(1) $h = 2A - b$
(2) $h = \frac{A}{2b}$
(3) $h = (2A)(b)$
(4) $h = \frac{2A}{b}$

Correct Answer: (4) $h = \frac{2A}{b}$. The formula of the area of a triangle is $A = \frac{1}{2} bh$. Multiplying both sides by 2 and dividing by b yields $h = \frac{2A}{b}$. *(Geometric Relationships)*

30. A set of five quadrilaterals consists of a square, a rhombus, a rectangle, an isosceles trapezoid, and a parallelogram. Lu selects one of these figures at random. What is the probability that both pairs of the figure's opposite sides are parallel?

(1) 1

(2) $\frac{4}{5}$

(3) $\frac{3}{4}$

(4) $\frac{2}{5}$

Correct Answer: (2) $\frac{4}{5}$. Out of these five shapes, four have opposite sides that are parallel (square, rhombus, rectangle, and parallelogram). The isosceles trapezoid has only one pair of parallel sides. Therefore, the answer is $\frac{4}{5}$. *(Shapes)*

---

31. A storage container in the shape of a right circular cylinder is shown in the accompanying diagram.

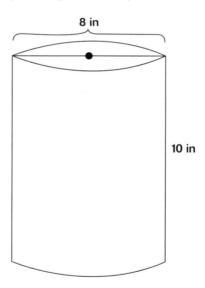

8 in

10 in

What is the volume of this container, to the *nearest hundredth?*

(1) 56.55 in³

(2) 125.66 in³

(3) 251.33 in³

(4) 502.65 in³

Correct Answer: (4) 502.65 in³. The volume of a right circular cylinder equals $\pi r^2 h$ where r represents the radius of the cylinder and h represents the height of the cylinder. *(Shapes)*

32. What is the length of one side of the square whose perimeter has the same numerical value as its area?

(1) 5
(2) 6
(3) 3
(4) 4

Correct Answer: (4) 4. Let x be the length of a side of the square, P = perimeter, A = area. Then $P = A$ implies that $4x = x^2$. Subtract $4x$ from both sides: $x^2 - 4x = 0$. Factor: $x(x - 4) = 0$. Set each factor equal to 0: $x = 0$ or $x = 4$. Reject $x = 0$ since a length cannot be 0. *(Geometric Relationships)*

33. If the midpoints of the sides of a triangle are connected, the area of the triangle formed is what part of the area of the original triangle?

(1) $\frac{1}{4}$
(2) $\frac{1}{3}$
(3) $\frac{3}{8}$
(4) $\frac{1}{2}$

Correct Answer: (1) By using segments connected to the midpoints, the base and the height of the triangle formed are cut in half. $\frac{1}{2} \times \frac{1}{2} = \frac{1}{4}$. *(Geometric Relationships)*

34. Delroy's sailboat has two sails that are similar triangles. The larger sail has sides of 10 feet, 24 feet, and 26 feet. If the shortest side of the smaller sail measures 6 feet, what is the perimeter of the *smaller* sail?

    (1) 15 ft
    (2) 36 ft
    (3) 60 ft
    (4) 100 ft

Correct Answer: (2) 36 ft.

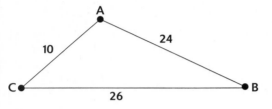 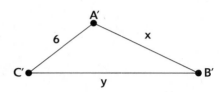

To find the perimeter, find the values of x and y by setting up two proportions, $\frac{10}{6} = \frac{24}{x}$. Cross-multiply: $10x = 144$. Divide both sides by 10: $x = 14.4$. $\overline{AB}$. Cross-multiply: $10y = 156$. Divide both sides by 10: $y = 15.6$. Let P = perimeter of triangle A'B'C'. $P = 6 + x + y = 6 + 14.4 + 15.6 = 36$ feet. *(Geometric Relationships)*

35. The coordinates of the point R are $(-3, 2)$ and the coordinates of point T are $(4, 1)$. What is the length of $\overline{RT}$?

    (1) $2\sqrt{2}$
    (2) $5\sqrt{2}$
    (3) $4\sqrt{3}$
    (4) $\sqrt{10}$

Correct Answer: (2) To find the length, use the distance formula: $d = \sqrt{\left(x - x_1\right)^2 + \left(y - y_1\right)^2}$. This yields $\sqrt{50} = \sqrt{25} \cdot \sqrt{2}$, and this is equal to $5\sqrt{2}$. *(Coordinate Geometry)*

36. If the measures of the angles of a triangle are represented by $2x$, $3x - 15$, and $7x + 15$, the triangle is

    (1) an isosceles triangle
    (2) a right triangle
    (3) an acute triangle
    (4) an equiangular triangle

Correct Answer: (1) an isosceles triangle. Since all three angles of a triangle must add up to 180°, set up the equation $2x + 3x - 15 + 7x + 15 = 180$. Combining like terms results in $12x = 180$. Dividing both sides by 12 results in $x = 15$. After plugging in $x = 15$ to each of the angle expressions, you find that this triangle has angles with measures of 30, 30, and 120. Since two angles have the same measure, this triangle is an isosceles triangle, choice (1). *(Shapes)*

37. The accompanying circle graph shows how Shannon earned $600 during her summer vacation.

    What is the measure of the central angle of the section labeled "Chores"?

    (1) 30°
    (2) 60°
    (3) 90°
    (4) 120°

Correct Answer: (2) 60°. Notice that the section labeled "Chores" makes an acute angle (less than 90°) so the correct choice must be (1) or (2). Since the "Chores" section represents $100 out of the total of $600, that is, 1/6 of the circle, the angle represents 1/6 of 360°, which equals 60°. *(Geometric Relationships)*

38. How many points are equidistant from two parallel lines and also equidistant from two points on one of the lines?

(1) 1
(2) 2
(3) 3
(4) 4

Correct Answer: (1) 1. The locus of points equidistant from two parallel lines is a parallel line in the middle of them the same distance from each line. The locus of points equidistant from two points is the perpendicular bisector. These two lines intersect in one and only one point. *(Locus)*

39. The second side of a triangle is two more inches than the first side, and the third side is three less inches than the first side. Which expression represents the perimeter of the triangle?

(1) $x + 5$
(2) $2x - 1$
(3) $3x - 1$
(4) $x^2 - x - 6$

Correct Answer: (3) $3x - 1$. Let x = length of the first side, $x + 2$ = length of the second side, and $x - 3$ = length of the third side. The perimeter of a figure is the sum of all its sides. So, the perimeter of this triangle is $x + x + 2 + x - 3 = 3x - 1$. *(Geometric Relationships)*

40. As shown in the accompanying diagram, the star in position 1 on a computer screen transforms to the star in position 2.

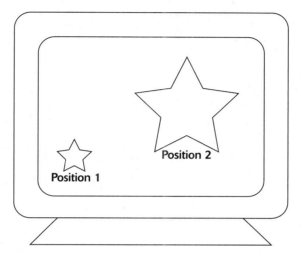

(1) line reflection
(2) translation
(3) rotation
(4) dilation

Correct Answer: (4) dilation. A dilation is a transformation that produces a change in size to the original object. None of the other choices produce a change in size. *(Transformational Geometry)*

41. Which phrase does *not* describe a triangle?

(1) acute scalene
(2) isosceles right
(3) equilateral equiangular
(4) obtuse right

Correct Answer: (4) obtuse right. A triangle's angles have a sum of 180°. A triangle cannot have an obtuse angle and a right angle because their sum would be greater than 180°. *(Geometric Relationships)*

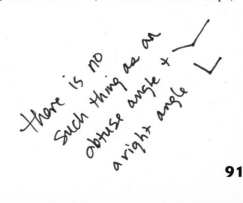

42. The accompanying diagram shows the roof of a house that is in the shape of an isosceles triangle. The vertex angle formed at the peak of the roof is 84°.

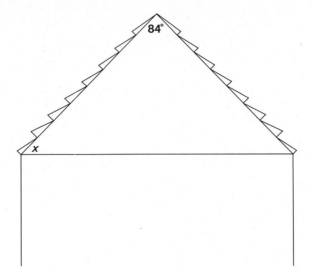

What is the measure of x?

(1) 138°

(2) 96°

(3) 84°

(4) 48°

Correct Answer: (4) 48°. Since the triangle is isosceles, the sides making up the vertex angle are congruent. This implies that the base angles are congruent, so each can be labeled x. Since in a triangle the sum of the angles is 180°, $x + x + 84 = 180 \rightarrow 2x + 84 = 180 \rightarrow 2x = 96 \rightarrow x = 48$. *(Geometric Relationships)*

43. In the accompanying diagram of $\triangle ABC$, $\overline{AB}$ is extended through D, $m\angle CBD = 30°$, and $\overline{AB} \cong \overline{BC}$.

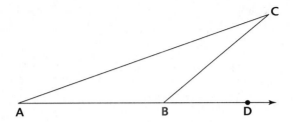

What is the measure of $\angle A$?

(1) 15°
(2) 30°
(3) 75°
(4) 150°

Correct Answer: (1) 15°. $\angle CBA = 180° - 30° = 150°$. In a triangle, the angles opposite congruent sides are congruent, so $\angle A \cong \angle B$. Since the angles in a triangle add up to 180° and $\angle CBA = 150°$, $\angle A + \angle B = 180° - 150° = 30°$. Since $\angle A \cong \angle B$, they each must equal 15°. *(Geometric Relationships)*

44. In the accompanying diagram, line ℓ_1 is parallel to line ℓ_2.

Which term describes the locus of all points that are equidistant from line ℓ_1 and line ℓ_2?

(1) line
(2) circle
(3) point
(4) rectangle

Correct Answer: (1) line. Draw a few points that are the same distance away from the two lines. You will notice that these points lie on a line parallel to the given lines and equidistant from both. *(Locus)*

45. The measures of two complementary angles are represented by $(3x + 15)$ and $(2x – 10)$. What is the value of x?

(1) 17
(2) 19
(3) 35
(4) 37

Correct Answer: (1) 17. Two complementary angles have a sum of 90°. $(3x + 15) + (2x – 10) = 90$. Combine like terms: $5x + 5 = 90$. Subtract from both sides: $5x = 85$. Divide both sides by 5: $x = 17$.

46. The accompanying circle graph shows how the Marino family spends its income each month.

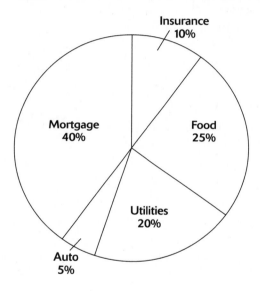

What is the measure, in degrees, of the central angle that represents the percentage of income spent on food?

(1) 25
(2) 50
(3) 90
(4) 360

Correct Answer: (3) 90. A circle contains 360°. Food is 25% of 360°, or $(.25)(360) = 90$. *(Geometric Relationships)*

47. The image of point (– 2, 3) under translation T is (3, –1). What is the image of point (4, 2) under the same translation?

   (1) (–1,6)

   (2) (0,7)

   (3) (5,4)

   (4) (9,–2)

Correct Answer: (4) (9,–2). Let $T_{(x,\,y)}$ = translation T. Since the image of (–2, 3) under $T_{(x,\,y)}$ yields (3, –1), it follows that –2 + x = 3. Add 2 to both sides: x = 5. And, 3 + y = –1. Subtract 3 from both sides: y = –4. The image of (4, 2) under $T_{(5,\,-4)}$ = (4 + 5, 2 + (–4)) = (9, –2). *(Transformational Geometry)*

48. In the accompanying diagram of parallelogram $ABCD$, diagonals $\overline{AC}$ and $\overline{BD}$ intersect at E, $BE = \frac{2}{3}x$ and $ED = x - 10$.

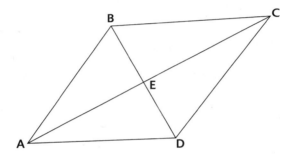

What is the value of x?

   (1) –30

   (2) 30

   (3) –6

   (4) 6

Correct Answer: (2) 30. In a parallelogram, the diagonals bisect each other. This implies that $x - 10 = \frac{2}{3}x$. Cross-multiply: $3x - 30 = 2x$. Subtract x from both sides: $-30 = -x$. Divide both sides by –1: $x = 30$. *(Geometric Relationships)*

49. What is the image of point (–3, 4) under the translation that shifts (*x*,*y*) to (*x* – 3, *y* + 2)?

    (1) (0,6)
    (2) (6,6)
    (3) (–6,8)
    (4) (–6,6)

Correct Answer: (4) (–6,6). The translation (*x* – 3, *y* + 2) means subtract 3 from *x* and add 2 to *y*. So, –3 – 3 = – 6 and 4 + 2 = 6. *(Transformational Geometry)*

50. Melissa is walking around the outside of a building that is in the shape of a regular polygon. She determines that the measure of one exterior angle of the building is 60°. How many sides does the building have?

    (1) 6
    (2) 9
    (3) 3
    (4) 12

Correct Answer: (1) 6. The exterior angles of a polygon add up to 360°. $\frac{360}{60}$ = 6. *(Shapes)*

51. On the banks of a river, surveyors marked locations *A*, *B*, and *C*. The measure of ∠*ACB* = 70° and the measure of ∠*ABC* = 65°.

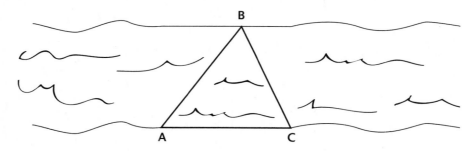

Which expression shows the relationship between the lengths of the sides of this triangle?

    (1) *AB* < *BC* < *AC*
    (2) *BC* < *AB* < *AC*
    (3) *BC* < *AC* < *AB*
    (4) *AC* < *AB* < *BC*

Correct Answer: (3) *BC* < *AC* < *AB*. In a triangle, the shortest side is opposite the smallest angle. Since *m*∠*ACB* + *m*∠*ABC* + *m*∠*BAC* = 180° and ∠*ACB* = 70° and ∠*ABC* = 65°, it follows that ∠*BAC* = 180° – 70° – 65° = 45°. In a triangle, the smallest side is opposite the smallest angle. Since *m*∠*BAC* < *m*∠*ABC* < ∠*ACB*, it follows that *BC* < *AC* < *AB*. *(Geometric Relationships)*

52. A builder is building a rectangular deck with dimensions of 16 feet by 30 feet. To ensure that the sides form 90° angles, what should each diagonal measure?

(1) 16 ft
(2) 30 ft
(3) 34 ft
(4) 46 ft

Correct Answer: (3) 34 ft. To ensure that the sides form 90° angles, two adjacent sides and the diagonal connecting them must form a right triangle in which you can apply the Pythagorean theorem. Here, the diagonal of the rectangle is the hypotenuse of the right triangle.

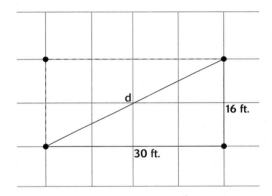

$16^2 + 30^2 = d^2 \rightarrow 256 + 900 = d^2 \rightarrow 1156 = d^2 \rightarrow \pm\sqrt{1156} = d \rightarrow \pm 34 = d$ (reject -34 since a dimension cannot be negative). The answer is $34 = d$. *(Geometric Relationships)*

53. The accompanying diagram shows two similar triangles.

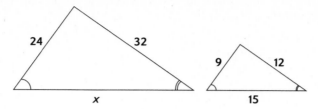

Which proportion could be used to solve for x?

(1) $\dfrac{x}{24} = \dfrac{9}{15}$

(2) $\dfrac{24}{9} = \dfrac{15}{x}$

(3) $\dfrac{32}{x} = \dfrac{12}{15}$

(4) $\dfrac{32}{12} = \dfrac{15}{x}$

Correct Answer: (3) $\dfrac{32}{x} = \dfrac{12}{15}$. If two triangles have two angles the same, then they are similar. In similar triangles the corresponding sides form a proportion. Corresponding sides are those that would overlap were you to superimpose the two triangles. 32 corresponds to 12; x corresponds to 15. *(Geometric Relationships)*

54. A farmer has a rectangular field that measures 100 feet by 150 feet. He plans to increase the area of the field by 20%. He will do this by increasing the length and width by the same amount, x. Which equation represents the area of the new field?

(1) $(100 + 2x)(150 + x) = 18,000$
(2) $2(100 + x) + 2(150 + x) = 15,000$
(3) $(100 + x)(150 + x) = 18,000$
(4) $(100 + x)(150 + x) = 15,000$

Correct Answer: (3) $(100 + x)(150 + x) = 18,000$. $A_{original\ rectangle}$ = (width)(length) = 100(150) = 15,000. The new rectangle's area must be larger by 20% so choices (2) and (4) are not correct. Since the width and length are increased by the same amount, x, the new width and length are $100 + x$ and $150 + x$, respectively. $A_{new\ rectangle} = (100 + x)(150 + x) = 15,000 + 20\%(15,000) = 18,000$. *(Geometric Relationships)*

55. A dog is tied with a rope to a stake in the ground. The length of the rope is 5 yards. What is the area, in square yards, in which the dog can roam?

(1) 25π
(2) 10π
(3) 25
(4) 20

Correct Answer: (1) 25π. The dog is moving in a circle, the center of which is at the stake in the ground. Since the length of the rope is 5 yards, the radius of the circle is 5 yards so $A = \pi r^2 = \pi(5)^2 = 25\pi$ square yards. *(Geometric Relationships)*

56. Which diagram represents the figure with the greatest volume?

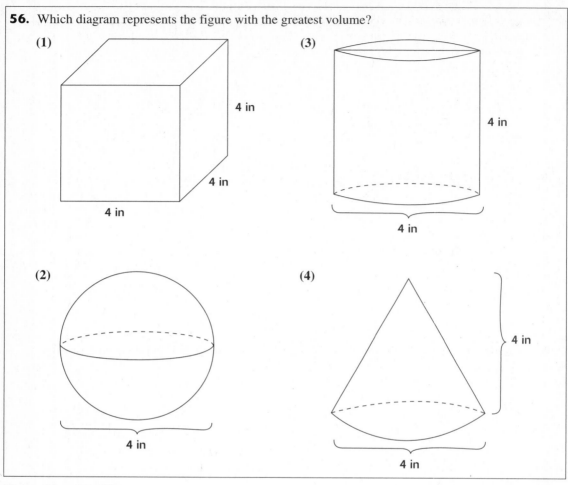

(1)

4 in

4 in

4 in

(3)

4 in

4 in

(2)

4 in

(4)

4 in

4 in

Correct Answer: (1)

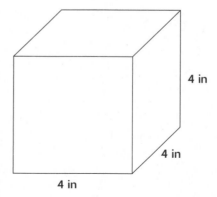

4 in

4 in

4 in

The cube has the greatest volume because the sphere, cone, and cylinder each fit inside it. *(Shapes)*

57. A box in the shape of a cube has a volume of 64 cubic inches. What is the length of a side of the box?

(1) $21.\overline{3}$ in
(2) 16 in
(3) 8 in
(4) 4 in

Correct Answer: (4) 4 in. $V_{box} = s^3 = 64$. Take the cube root of both sides: $x = 4$. *(Shapes)*

58. In the accompanying diagram, point *P* lies 3 centimeters from line ℓ.

How many points are both 2 centimeters from line ℓ and 1 centimeter from point *P*?

(1) 1
(2) 2
(3) 0
(4) 4

Correct Answer: (1) 1. The locus of points 2 centimeters away from line ℓ are two lines parallel to line ℓ. The locus of points 1 centimeter away from point *P* is a circle of radius 1 with center at *P*. The two loci—the circle and the two lines—intersect at only one point. *(Locus)*

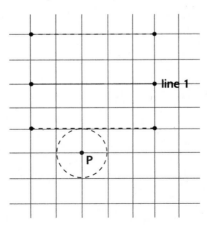

59. Which graph is symmetric with respect to the *y*-axis?

(1)

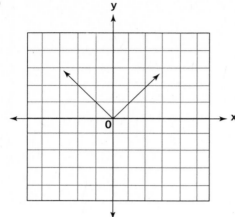

(3)

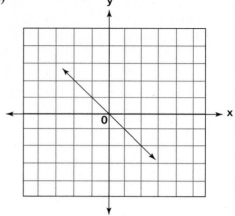

(2)

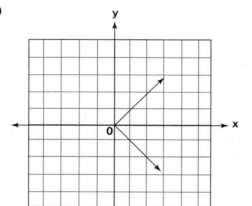

(4)

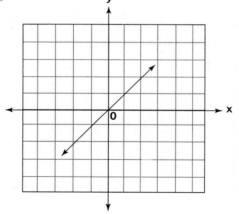

Correct Answer: (1)

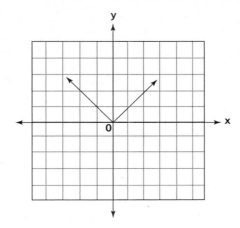

The graph in choice (1) is symmetric with respect to the *y*-axis because the *y*-axis acts as a mirror for the graph—that is, when the left side of the graph mirrors in the *y*-axis, it yields the right side of the graph. *(Transformational Geometry)*

---

60. The ratio of two supplementary angles is 3:6. What is the measure of the smaller angle?

    (1) 10°
    (2) 20°
    (3) 30°
    (4) 60°

Correct Answer: (4) 60°. Let $3x$ = the smaller angle; let $6x$ = the larger angle. Since they are supplementary, $3x + 6x = 180° \rightarrow 9x = 180°$. Divide by 9 on both sides: $x = 20° \rightarrow 3x = 60°$. *(Geometric Relationships)*

61. Which transformation does *not* always result in an image that is congruent to the original figure?

    (1) dilation
    (2) reflection
    (3) rotation
    (4) translation

Correct Answer: (1) dilation. A dilation enlarges or shrinks a figure so the image of a figure under a dilation is smaller or larger—except in the trivial case in which the dilation factor is 1 and the figure does not change size. *(Transformational Geometry)*

62. Triangle *ABC* represents a metal flag on pole *AD*, as shown in the accompanying diagram. On a windy day, the triangle spins around the pole so fast that it looks like a three-dimensional shape.

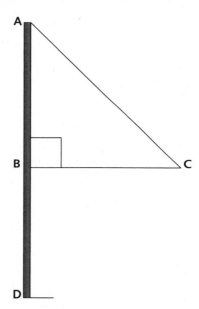

Which shape would the spinning flag create?

    (1) sphere
    (2) pyramid
    (3) right circular cylinder
    (4) cone

Correct Answer: (4) cone. As the triangle spins 360°, point *C* forms a circular base. From the four choices, only the shapes in choices (3) and (4) have circular bases. Point *A* does not move, thus creating an apex, (a sharp corner). This describes a cone. *(Shapes)*

63. A stop sign in the shape of a regular octagon is resting on a brick wall, as shown in the accompanying diagram.

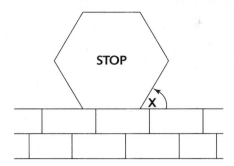

What is the measure of angle *x*?

(1) 45°
(2) 60°
(3) 120°
(4) 135°

Correct Answer: (1) To find the measure of each interior angle of a regular polygon, first find the sum of all the angles by $(n - 2)180°$, where n = the number of sides, which in this problem is 8. The sum of all the angles equals 1080°, and each interior angle is equal to $\left(\frac{1080}{8} = 135° \right)$. Then 108° − 135° = 45°. *(Shapes)*

64. In the accompanying graph, if point P has coordinates (a, b), which point has coordinates $(-b, a)$?

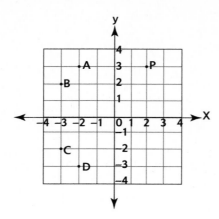

(1) A
(2) B
(3) C
(4) D

Correct Answer: (2) B. To change (a, b) to $(-b, a)$, you need to switch the coordinates and negate the x-coordinate. This is done when a point is rotated 90° clockwise. If point P is rotated this way, it ends up at point B. *(Transformational Geometry)*

65. In the accompanying diagram, line *l* is parallel to line *m*, and line *t* is a transversal.

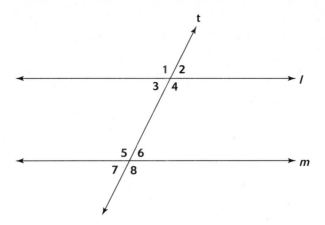

Which must be a true statement?

(1) $m\angle 1 + m\angle 4 = 180$
(2) $m\angle 1 + m\angle 8 = 180$
(3) $m\angle 3 + m\angle 6 = 180$
(4) $m\angle 2 + m\angle 5 = 180$

Correct Answer: (4) $m\angle 2 + m\angle 5 = 180$. When two parallel lines are intersected by a transversal, the sum of any acute angle and any obtuse angle is 180°. *(Geometric Relationships)*

66. In the accompanying diagram of a construction, what does $\overline{PC}$ represent?

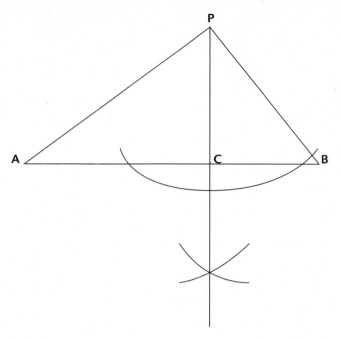

    (1) an altitude drawn to $\overline{AB}$
    (2) a median drawn to $\overline{AB}$
    (3) the bisector of $\angle APB$
    (4) the perpendicular bisector of $\overline{AB}$

Correct Answer: (1) an altitude drawn to $\overline{AB}$. The drawing represents a perpendicular being drawn to the base of a triangle from the opposite vertex—this is a definition for an altitude of a triangle. *(Constructions)*

67. $\overline{AB}$ and $\overline{CD}$ intersect at point E, $m\angle AEC = 6x + 20$, and $m\angle DEB = 10x$. What is the value of x?
    (1) $4\frac{3}{8}$
    (2) 5
    (3) 10
    (4) $21\frac{1}{4}$

Correct Answer: (2) 5. The given angles are vertical and, thus, equal in measure: $6x + 20 = 10x$. Subtract $6x$ from both sides: $20 = 4x$. Divide both sides by 4: $x = 5$. *(Geometric Relationships)*

68. In the coordinate plane, the points (2,2) and (2,12) are the endpoints of a diameter of a circle. What is the length of the radius of the circle?

   (1) 5

   (2) 6

   (3) 7

   (4) 10

Correct Answer: (1) 5. If you plot the given points, you will find that the distance between them, the length of the diameter of the circle, is 10 units. The radius is 5 units since it equals half of the diameter. *(Coordinate Geometry)*

69. The measures of two consecutive angles of a parallelogram are in the ratio 5:4. What is the measure of an obtuse angle of the parallelogram?

   (1) 20°

   (2) 80°

   (3) 100°

   (4) 160°

Correct Answer: (3) 100°. In a parallelogram, consecutive angles are supplementary, that is, they add up to 180°. Let $5x =$ one angle, $4x =$ the other angle. Then, $5x + 4x = 180 \rightarrow 9x = 180 \rightarrow x = 20$. $5x = 5(20) = 100$, $4x = 4(20) = 80$. The obtuse angle is 100°. *(Geometric Relationships)*

70. Which equation represents the locus of all points 5 units below the x-axis?

   (1) $x = -5$

   (2) $x = 5$

   (3) $y = -5$

   (4) $y = 5$

Correct Answer: (3) $y = -5$. The equation $x =$ a constant and is a vertical line, and the line 5 units below the x-axis is a horizontal line. The equation $y =$ a constant and is a horizontal line that is parallel to the x-axis. 5 units below would be a negative value, so choice 3 is the answer. *(Locus)*

71. The coordinates of A are (−9, 2), and the coordinates of G are (3, 14). What are the coordinates of the midpoint of $\overline{AG}$?

   (1) (−3,8)

   (2) (−6,6)

   (3) (−6,16)

   (4) (−21,−10)

Correct Answer: (1) (−3,8). The midpoint of a line segment with endpoints (x_1, y_1) and (x_2, y_2) is given by $\left(\dfrac{x_1 + x_2}{2}, \dfrac{y_1 + y_2}{2} \right) = \left(\dfrac{-9 + 3}{2}, \dfrac{2 + 14}{2} \right) = \left(\dfrac{-6}{2}, \dfrac{16}{2} \right) = (-3,8)$. *(Coordinate Geometry)*

72. What are the coordinates of P', the image of P $(-4, 0)$ under the translation $(x - 3, y + 6)$?

    (1) $(-7,6)$
    (2) $(7,-6)$
    (3) $(1,6)$
    (4) $(2,-3)$

Correct Answer: (1) $(-7,6)$. $(x - 3, y + 6) = (-4 - 3, 0 + 6) = (-7,6)$. *(Transformational Geometry)*

73. What is the total number of points of intersection of the graphs of the equations $x^2 + y^2 = 16$ and $y = x$?

    (1) 1
    (2) 2
    (3) 3
    (4) 4

Correct Answer: (2) 2. Draw the circle and line. $x^2 + y^2 = 16$ is a circle with center at origin and radius of 4. $y = x$ is a line through the origin with a slope of 1. They have two intersection points. *(Geometric Relationships)*

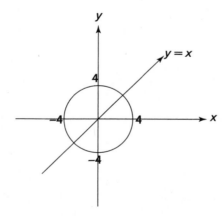

74. A line segment on the coordinate plane has endpoints (2,4) and (4,y). The midpoint of the segment is point (3,7). What is the value of y?

(1) 11
(2) 10
(3) 5
(4) –2

Correct Answer: (2) 10. The midpoint is halfway between two endpoints. If two endpoints are (x_1,y_1) and (x_2,y_2), then the midpoint is $\left(\dfrac{x_1+x_2}{2}, \dfrac{y_1+y_2}{2}\right)$. If the midpoint is given and an endpoint is missing, then double the midpoint so (3, 7) becomes (6, 14) and subtract the given endpoint from the corresponding coordinates, so (6, 14) – (2, 4) is (4, 10). The missing endpoint is (4, 10) and $y = 10$. *(Coordinate Geometry)*

75. What is the image of point (–3,–1) under a reflection in the origin?

(1) (3,1)
(2) (–3,1)
(3) (1,3)
(4) (–1,–3)

Correct Answer: (1) (3,1). When reflecting a point in the origin, the x and y values are negated. *(Transformational Geometry)*

76. In a certain quadrilateral, two opposite sides are parallel, and the other two opposite sides are *not* congruent. This quadrilateral could be a

(1) rhombus
(2) parallelogram
(3) square
(4) trapezoid

Correct Answer: (4) trapezoid. All parallelograms, which include the square and rhombus have both pairs of opposite sides congruent. Therefore, the only choice left is a trapezoid. Trapezoids have one pair of parallel sides, and the non-parallel sides could be congruent or non-congruent. *(Shapes)*

77. The accompanying diagram shows a football player crossing the 20-yard line at an angle of 30° and continuing along the same path.

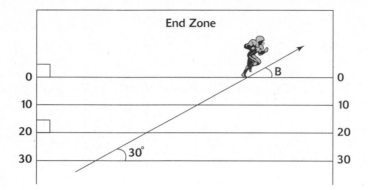

What is the measure of angle *B*, where the player crosses into the end zone?

(1) 30°
(2) 60°
(3) 150°
(4) 180°

Correct Answer: (1) 30°. The football player's path is a transversal that intersects four parallel lines. Angle B and the angle with a measure of 30° are corresponding angles and, hence, are equal in measure. *(Geometric Relationships)*

78. Which letter demonstrates line symmetry but *not* point symmetry?

(1) T
(2) N
(3) H
(4) S

Correct Answer: (1) T. Line symmetry is when you can draw a line through the letter, and the two halves are the same or mirror images of each other. When you draw a vertical line through the middle of T, each half is the mirror image of the other. When you rotate T 180° around a fixed point, it will not be in the same position. *(Transformational Geometry)*

79. Which set *cannot* represent the lengths of the sides of a triangle?

    (1) {4,5,6}
    (2) {5,5,11}
    (3) {7,7,12}
    (4) {8,8,8}

Correct Answer: (2) {5,5,11}. In a triangle, the sum of any two sides must be greater or equal to the third side. Since $5 + 5 = 10$ and 10 is not greater than 11, the sides of a triangle cannot be {5, 5, 11}. *(Shapes)*

80. Sara is building a triangular pen for her pet rabbit. If two of the sides measure 8 feet and 15 feet, the length of the third side could be

    (1) 13 ft
    (2) 7 ft
    (3) 3 ft
    (4) 23 ft

Correct Answer: (1) 13 ft. When figuring a possible third side of a triangle use the Triangle Inequality, which states that the sum of any two sides of a triangle must be greater than the third side. The best way to do this is to add the two sides given and subtract the two sides given. The third side must be a number in between those two answers. $8 + 15 = 23$ and $15 - 8 = 7$. 13 ft is the only one in between 7 and 23. The third side cannot be 7 or 23. *(Geometric Relationships)*

81. Which equation represents the locus of points 4 units from the origin?

   (1) $x = 4$
   (2) $x^2 + y^2 = 4$
   (3) $x + y = 16$
   (4) $x^2 + y^2 = 16$

Correct Answer: (4) $x^2 + y^2 = 16$.

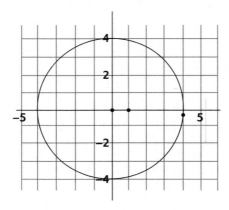

The locus of all points 4 units from the origin is a circle of radius 4 with center at the origin. *(Locus)*

82. What is the converse of the statement "If Alicia goes to Albany, then Ben goes to Buffalo"?

   (1) If Alicia does not go to Albany, then Ben does not go to Buffalo.
   (2) Alicia goes to Albany if and only if Ben goes to Buffalo.
   (3) If Ben goes to Buffalo, then Alicia goes to Albany.
   (4) If Ben does not go to Buffalo, then Alicia does not go to Albany.

Correct Answer: (3) If Ben goes to Buffalo, then Alicia goes to Albany. The converse of a statement is when the hypothesis (first part of the statement) and conclusion (last part of the statement) switch places. This is choice (3). *(Informal Proof)*

83. What is the sum, in degrees, of the measures of the interior angles of a stop sign, which is in the shape of an octagon?

    (1) 360
    (2) 1,080
    (3) 1,440
    (4) 1,880

Correct Answer: (2) 1,080. The sum of the measures of the interior angles of a polygon = $180(n - 2)$ where n = the number of sides of the polygon. In this case, $180(n - 2) = 180(8 - 2) = 180(6) = 1080$. *(Shapes)*

84. The graph of the equation $x^2 + y^2 = 4$ can be described as a

    (1) line passing through points $(0, 2)$ and $(2, 0)$.
    (2) parabola with its vertex at $(0, 2)$.
    (3) circle with its center at the origin and a radius of 2.
    (4) circle with its center at the origin and a radius of 4.

Correct Answer: (3) The equation of a circle with the center at the origin is $x^2 + y^2 = r^2$, where r = radius. In the problem, $r^2 = 4$, so $r = 2$. *(Coordinate Geometry)*

85. When solved graphically, which system of equations will have *exactly* one point of intersection?

    (1) $y = -x - 20$
        $y = x + 17$
    (2) $y = 0.5x + 30$
        $y = 0.5x - 30$
    (3) $\frac{1}{2} bh$
        $y = 0.6x - 19$
    (4) $y = -x + 15$
        $y = -x + 25$

Correct Answer: (1) Go to $y =$ on a graphing calculator and type one equation in Y1 and the other in Y2. Graph and look at the point(s) of intersection, if any. Choice (1) has only one intersection point. All the others are parallel. *(Coordinate Geometry)*

Open-Ended Questions

> **86.** Two angles are complementary. One angle has a measure that is five times the measure of the other angle. What is the measure, in degrees, of the larger angle?

Correct Answer: 75°. Let x = the measure of the smaller angle; then $5x$ = the measure of the larger angle. Complementary angles have a sum of 90°, so $x + 5x = 90 \rightarrow 6x = 90 \rightarrow x = 15$. The larger angle is $5x = 5(15) = 75°$. *(Shapes)*

> **87.** $\overleftrightarrow{AB}$ and $\overleftrightarrow{CD}$ intersect at E. If $m\angle AEC = 5x - 20$ and $m\angle BED = x + 50$, find, in degrees, $m\angle CEB$.

Correct Answer: $m\angle CEB = 112.5°$. When two lines intersect, the opposite angles, called vertical angles, are congruent.

$5x - 20 = x + 50$. Subtract x from both sides and add 20 to both sides: $4x = 70$. Divide both sides by 4: $x = 17.5$. $m\angle AEC = 5x - 20 = 5(17.5) - 20 = 67.5$. $m\angle CEB$ and $m\angle AEC$ are supplementary, so they add up to 180°. $m\angle CEB = 180 - 67.5 = 112.5°$. *(Geometric Relationships)*

> **88.** A wheel has a radius of 5 feet. What is the minimum number of *complete* revolutions that the wheel must make to roll at least 1,000 feet?

Correct Answer: The minimum number of complete revolutions in order to cover 1000 feet is 32.

One complete revolution is equivalent to the circumference of the wheel, $C = 2\pi r = 2\pi(5) = 10\pi$ feet = 31.415 feet. To calculate how many revolutions it will take to reach at least 1,000 feet, $\frac{1000}{31.415} = 31.8 \approx 32$ revolutions. *(Geometric Relationships)*

89. Dylan says that all isosceles triangles are acute triangles. Mary Lou wants to prove that Dylan is *not* correct. Sketch an isosceles triangle that Mary Lou could use to show that Dylan's statement is not true. In your sketch, state the measure of *each* angle of the isosceles triangle.

Correct Answer:

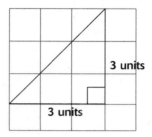

This is an example of an isosceles right triangle. *(Shapes)*

90. In the accompanying diagram of $\triangle BCD$, $m\angle C = 70$, $m\angle CDE = 130$, and side $\overline{BD}$ is extended to A and to E. Find $m\angle CBA$.

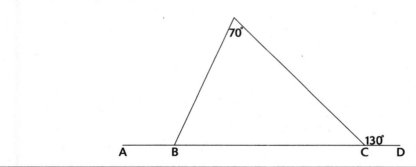

Correct Answer: $m\angle CBA = 120°$; $m\angle CBA = m\angle C + m\angle CDB$. $m\angle CDB = 180° - 130° = 50°$. $m\angle CBA = 70° + 50°$. *(Geometric Relationships)*

91. Triangle *ABC* has coordinates *A*(2,0), *B*(1,7), and *C*(5,1). On the accompanying set of axes, graph, label, and state the coordinates of △A'B'C', the reflection of △*ABC* in the *y*-axis.

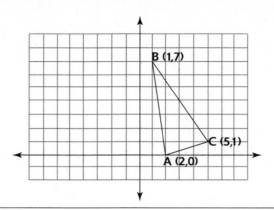

Correct Answer:

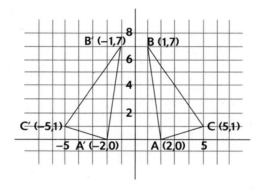

To reflect a point in the *y*-axis, negate the *x*-coordinate and leave the *y*-coordinate the same. A'(−2,0), B'(−1,7), C'(−5,1). *(Transformational Geometry)*

92. The coordinates of the midpoint of $\overline{AB}$ are (2,4), and the coordinates of point B are (3,7). What are the coordinates of point A? (The use of the accompanying grid is optional.)

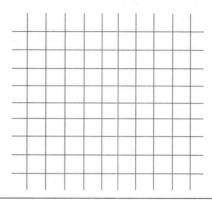

Correct Answer: $A(1, 1)$.

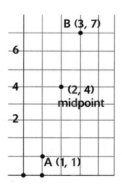

Let $A(x, y)$. Then $(2,4) = \left(\dfrac{3 + x}{2}, \dfrac{7 + y}{2} \right) \rightarrow 2 = \dfrac{3 + x}{2}$. Cross-multiply and subtract 3 from both sides: $x = 1$. $4 = \dfrac{7 + y}{2}$. Cross-multiple and subtract 7 from both sides: $y = 1$. *(Coordinate Geometry)*

93. In the accompanying diagram, the perimeter of △*MNO* is equal to the perimeter of square *ABCD*. If the sides of the triangle are represented by $4x + 4$, $5x - 3$, and 17, and one side of the square is represented by $3x$, find the length of a side of the square.

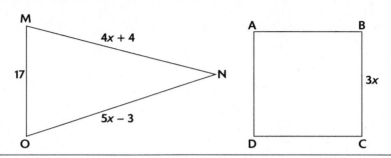

Correct Answer: 18. To find the perimeter of a polygon, you add up all the sides. When you add up the sides of the triangle, you get $4x + 4 + 5x - 3 + 17$. This simplifies to $9x + 18$. All sides of a square are equal so if one side is $3x$, then they all are. All the sides of the square add to $12x$. Now set the two perimeters equal to each other to get $9x + 18 = 12x$. Solve this equation to get $x = 6$. One side of the square is $3x$ so $3(6) = 18$. One side of the square is 18. *(Shapes)*

94. Using only a compass and a straightedge, construct the perpendicular bisector of $\overline{AB}$ and label it *c*. (Leave all construction marks.)

Correct Answer:

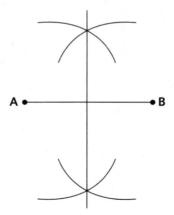

Draw the circle centered at *A* and passing through *B*. Draw the circle centered at *B* and passing through *A*. The two circles intersect at two points. Draw the line through these two points. This line is the perpendicular bisector to *AB*. *(Constructions)*

95. The accompanying circle graph shows the favorite colors of the 300 students in the ninth grade. How many students chose red as their favorite color?

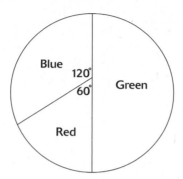

Correct Answer: 50 students chose red. $\frac{60°}{360°} = \frac{1}{6}$; $\frac{1}{6} \cdot 300 = 50$. *(Shapes)*

96. In the accompanying diagram of right triangles ABD and DBC, $AB = 5$, $AD = 4$, and $CD = 1$. Find the length of $\overline{BC}$ to the *nearest tenth*.

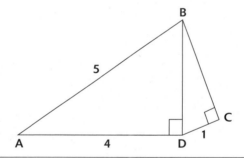

Correct Answer: $\overline{BC} = 2.8$.

Use the Pythagorean theorem to find the length of side BD.
$4^2 + (BD)^2 = 5^2$. Subtract 4^2 from both sides: $(BD)^2 = 5^2 - 4^2 = 9$.
Take the square root of both sides: $BD = \pm 3$. Reject $BD = -3$ since a length cannot be negative. $BD = 3$.
Use the Pythagorean theorem again to find the length of BC. $1^2 + 3^2 = (BC)^2$
$10 = (BC)^2$. Take the square root of both sides: $\pm \sqrt{10} = BC$. Reject $-\sqrt{10}$, $BC = \sqrt{10} = 2.8$. *(Geometric Relationships)*

97. Express both the perimeter and the area of the rectangle shown in the accompanying diagram as polynomials in simplest form.

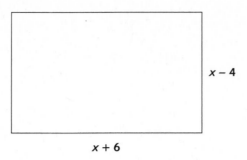

$x - 4$

$x + 6$

Correct Answer: $P = 4x + 4$, $A = x^2 + 2x - 24$; $P = 2L + 2W = 2(x + 6) + 2(x - 4) = 4x + 4$.
$A = L \times W = (x + 6)(x - 4) = x^2 + 2x - 24$. *(Geometric Relationships)*

98. In the accompanying diagram, $\overleftrightarrow{CD} \parallel \overleftrightarrow{EF}$, $\overleftrightarrow{AB}$ is a transversal, $m\angle DGH = 2x$, and $m\angle FHB = 5x - 51$. Find the measure, in degrees, of $\angle BHE$.

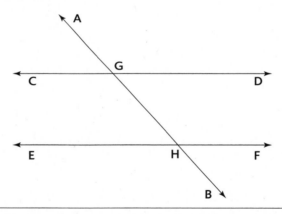

Correct Answer: Angles *DGH* and *FHB* are corresponding angles, so they are equal. Thus, $2x = 5x - 51$. Subtract $5x$ from both sides: $2x - 5x = -51 \rightarrow -3x = -51$. Divide both sides by -3: $x = 17 \rightarrow m\angle FHB = 5(17) - 51 = 34° \rightarrow m\angle BHE = 180° - 34° = 146°$. *(Geometric Relationships)*

99. In the accompanying diagram, right triangle ABC is inscribed in circle O, diameter $AB = 26$, and $CB = 10$. Find, to the *nearest square unit*, the area of the shaded region.

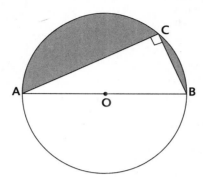

Correct Answer: $A_{shaded} = 145$. $A_{shaded} = A_{semicircle} - A_{triangle}$. $A_{semicircle} = \frac{1}{2}\pi r^2 = \frac{1}{2}\pi(13)^2 = \frac{169\pi}{2}$. Since BC and AC are perpendicular to each other, they are the triangle's height and base. $A_{triangle} = \frac{1}{2}bh = \frac{1}{2}(BC)(AC)$. To find the measure of AC, use the Pythagorean theorem: $(AC)^2 + (BC)^2 = (AB)^2 \rightarrow (AC)^2 + 10^2 = 26^2 \rightarrow (AC)^2 = 26^2 - 10^2 = 576 \rightarrow AC = \sqrt{576} = 24$. $A_{triangle} = \frac{1}{2}(BC)(AC) = \frac{1}{2}(10)(24) = 120$. $A_{shaded} = \frac{169\pi}{2} - 120 \approx 145$. *(Shapes)*

---

100. In $\triangle ABC$, the measure of $\angle B$ is 21 less than four times the measure of $\angle A$, and the measure of $\angle C$ is 1 more than five times the measure of $\angle A$. Find the measure, in degrees, of *each* angle of $\triangle ABC$.

Correct Answer: $\angle A = 20°$, $\angle B = 59°$, $\angle C = 101°$ Since the other two angles are being compared to $\angle A$ it should be given a value of x. With that, $\angle B = 4x - 21$ and $\angle C = 5x + 1$, and since a triangle has $180°$, the equation to find the angles would be $x + 4x - 21 + 5x + 1 = 180$. This yields $x = 20$, and this is plugged in to determine the three angles. *(Shapes)*

---

101. Determine the area, in square feet, of the *smallest* square that can contain a circle with a radius of 8 feet.

Correct Answer: 256 square feet. The smallest square containing this circle must have the circle inscribed in it. In this case, the diameter of the circle, which is 16 feet, is equal to the length of a side of the square. Then, the area of the square is $(16\ ft)^2$ or 256 square feet. *(Geometric Relationships)*

102. Mr. Petri has a rectangular plot of land with length = 20 feet and width = 10 feet. He wants to design a flower garden in the shape of a circle with two semicircles at each end of the center circle, as shown in the accompanying diagram. He will fill in the shaded area with wood chips. If one bag of wood chips covers 5 square feet, how many bags must he buy?

20 ft

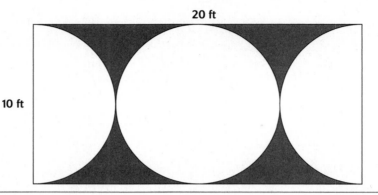

10 ft

Correct Answer: 9. This is an area problem. To find the area to be covered in wood chips, you must find the area of the rectangular area and subtract out the areas of the circle and 2 semicircles. The area of the rectangle is (a = length × width) so the area = (20)(10), which is 200 ft². The diameter of each circle or semicircle is the same as the width of the rectangle, which is 10 feet. The radius of a circle is half the diameter so the radius equals 5 feet. The two semicircles have the same diameter so the two of them together make one circle. Both circles have the same diameter so their areas are the same. The area of a circle is ($A = \pi r^2$) so the area of one circle equals $\pi(5)^2$, which is 78.5398 ft². Both circles have a combined area of 157. 0796 ft². The wood chip area is 200 − 157.0796, which is 42.9204 ft². If one bag covers 5 square feet, then to find the number of bags to cover the area divide the area by 5 to get 8.584 bags, which rounds to 9 bags. You probably wouldn't be able to buy part of a bag so that's why you round to 9. *(Shapes)*

103. As shown in the accompanying diagram, the length, width, and height of Richard's fish tank are 24 inches, 16 inches, 18 inches, respectively. Richard is filling his fish tank with water from a hose at the rate of 500 cubic inches per minute. How long will it take, to the nearest minute, to fill the tank to a depth of 15 inches?

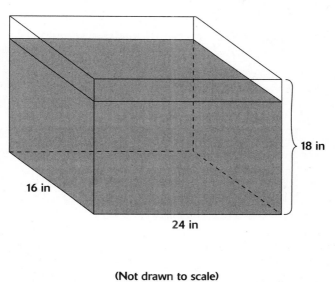

18 in

16 in

24 in

(Not drawn to scale)

Correct Answer: 12 minutes. The fact that the tank is 18 inches deep is not significant. The height needed is 15 inches. To find the volume, use $V = lwh$, where $l = 24$ inches, $w = 16$ inches, and $h = 15$ inches. The volume is 5,760 inches^3 and dividing that by the rate of 500 inches^3 / minute yields 11.52 minutes. Rounded to the nearest minute is 12 minutes. *(Shapes)*

104. Two hikers started at the same location. One traveled 2 miles east and then 1 mile north. The other traveled 1 mile west and then 3 miles south. At the end of their hikes, how many miles apart are the two hikers?

Correct Answer: 5 miles.

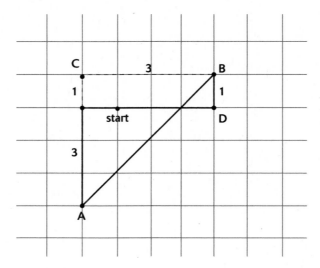

Pick any point on the grid. Move 2 units east (to the right) and 1 unit north (up). This is where the first hiker ends. From the same starting point move 1 unit west (to the left) and 3 units south (down). This is where the second hiker ends. The length connecting these endpoints is 5 miles since it is the hypotenuse of a right triangle with legs 3 miles and 4 miles.

105. Dan is sketching a map of the location of his house and his friend Matthew's house on a set of coordinate axes. Dan locates his house at point $D(0,0)$ and locates Matthew's house, which is 6 miles east of Dan's house, at point $M(6,0)$. On the accompanying set of coordinate axes, graph the locus of points equidistant from the two houses. Then write the equation of the locus.

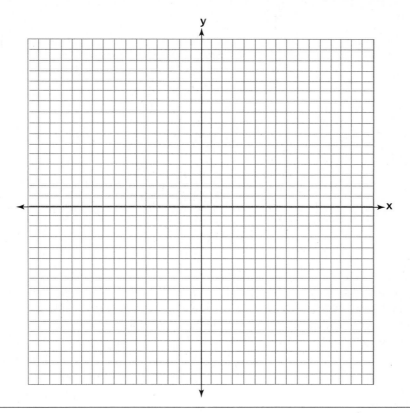

Correct Answer: $x = 3$. The locus of points equidistant from two points lie on a line perpendicular to the segment connecting the two points. The equation of the locus of points is $x = 3$. *(Locus)*

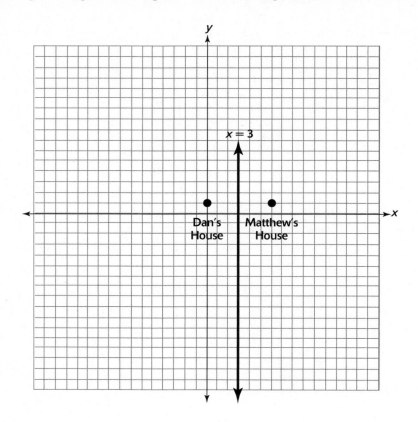

106. On the accompanying square, draw all the lines of symmetry.

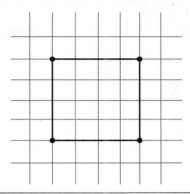

Correct Answer:

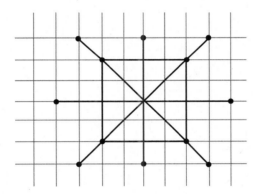

(Constructions)

107. Jose wants to build a triangular pen for his pet rabbit. He has three lengths of boards already cut that measure 7 feet, 8 feet, and 16 feet. Explain why Jose cannot construct a pen in the shape of a triangle with sides of 7 feet, 8 feet, and 16 feet.

Correct Answer: Triangle Inequality Theorem. The sum of the 2 smaller sides of a triangle must be greater than the length of the third side. In this case, $7 + 8 = 15$, which is less than 16, so this is not a triangle. *(Geometric Relationships)*

108. On the accompanying set of axes, draw the reflection of *ABCD* on the *y*-axis. Label and state the coordinates of the reflected figure.

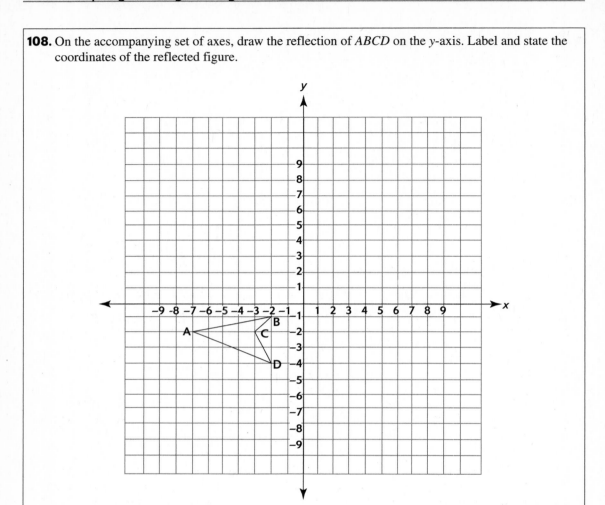

Correct Answer: Coordinates of *A'B'C'D'* are (7, –2), (2, –1), (3, –2), (2, –4). When reflecting points over the *y*-axis, the *x*-coordinate gets negated, and the *y*-coordinate of the original figure remains the same. For example: *A* is (–7, –2) so *A'* is (7, –2). *(Transformational Geometry)*

109. Manuel plans to install a fence around the perimeter of his yard. His yard is shaped like a square and has an area of 40,000 square feet. The company that he hires charges $2.50 per foot for the fencing and $50.00 for the installation fee. What will be the cost of the fence, in dollars?

Correct Answer: The cost of fence will be $2,050. Since the yard is square, its sides are all equal in length; call this length x. Since the area is 40,000 square feet, $x^2 = 40,000$. Take the square root of both sides: $x = \pm 200$ (reject -200 since a length cannot be negative); $x = 200$ feet. Since each side is 200 feet, the perimeter is $200(4) = 800$ ft. For each of these feet the price is $2.50 \rightarrow 2.50(800) = \$2,000$. You must add to this the installation fee of $50 to reach a total cost of $2,050.

110. In a circle whose center is (2,3), one endpoint of a diameter is (–1,5). Find the coordinates of the other endpoint of that diameter.

Correct Answer: (5,1). The center of a circle is the midpoint of a diameter. Let one endpoint be $(x_1, y_1) = (-1, 5)$ and the other endpoint be $(x_2, y_2) = (x, y)$. Then, $\left(\dfrac{x_1 + x_2}{2}, \dfrac{y_1 + y_2}{2} \right) = \left(\dfrac{-1 + x}{2}, \dfrac{5 + y}{2} \right) = \left(\dfrac{-1 + x}{2}, \dfrac{5 + y}{2} \right) = (2, 3)$. This implies: $\dfrac{-1 + x}{2} = 2$. Multiply both sides by 2: $-1 + x = 4$. Add 1 to both sides: $x = 5$. Also $\dfrac{5 + y}{2} = 3$. Multiply both sides by 2: $5 + y = 6$. Subtract 5 from both sides: $y = 1$. *(Coordinate Geometry)*

111. In rectangle $ABCD$, $AC = 3x + 15$ and $BD = 4x - 5$. Find the length of $\overline{AC}$.

Correct Answer: 75. In rectangle $ABCD$, AC and BD represent the diagonals, which are congruent by the definition of a rectangle. Setting the two equal to each other: $3x + 15 = 4x - 5$, yields $x = 20$. Plugging in 20 for x into the equation for AC gives the length, which is 75. *(Shapes)*

112. Mr. James wanted to plant a garden that would be in the shape of a rectangle. He was given 80 feet of fencing to enclose his garden. He wants the length to be 10 feet more than twice the width. What are the dimensions, in feet, for a rectangular garden that will use exactly 80 feet of fencing?

Correct Answer: 10 ft. × 30 ft. garden. Let the width equal w. Let the length equal $2w + 10$. Since this is a perimeter problem, set up the equation $w + w + 2w + 10 + 2w + 10 = 80$. Solve and get $w = 10$ ft. The length will then equal $2(10) + 10$, which is 30 ft. *(Shapes)*

Measurement

Multiple-Choice Questions

---

1. A circular garden has a diameter of 12 feet. How many bags of topsoil must Linda buy to cover the garden if one bag covers an area of 3 square feet?

  (1) 13
  (2) 38
  (3) 40
  (4) 151

Correct Answer: (2) 38. Since the diameter = 12 feet, the radius = 6 feet. Since $A = \pi r^2$, the area of this circle is 36π square feet. You must divide 36π by 3 in order to calculate the number of necessary topsoil bags. Since you cannot purchase part of a bag, round up to 38 to ensure the entire area is covered. *(Tools and Methods)*

---

2. A bicyclist leaves Bay Shore traveling at an average speed of 12 miles per hour. Three hours later, a car leaves Bay Shore, on the same route, traveling at an average speed of 30 miles per hour. How many hours after the car leaves Bay Shore will the car catch up to the cyclist?

  (1) 8
  (2) 2
  (3) 5
  (4) 4

Correct Answer: (2) 2. Remember the formula $d = rt$ where d =distance, r = rate, t = time. If x = time traveled by bicyclist and $x - 3$ = time traveled by car (because the car leaves 3 hours later), use the equation $12x = 30(x - 3)$. You want to know when the two have traveled the same distance. Solve the equation and $x = 5$, which is the time for the bicyclist and $x - 3 = 2$, which is the time for the car. By then both have gone 60 miles, and they're equal. *(Units of Measurement)*

3. A triangle has sides whose lengths are 5, 12, and 13. A similar triangle could have sides with lengths of

   (1) 3, 4, and 5
   (2) 6, 8, and 10
   (3) 7, 24, and 25
   (4) 10, 24, and 26

Correct Answer: (4) Similar triangles have sides that are in proportion. Doubling each side of the original triangle will yield sides of 10, 24, and 26. (*Similar Figures*)

4. Triangle *A'B'C'* is the image of △*ABC* under a dilation such that *A'B'* = 3*AB*. Triangles *ABC* and *A'B'C'* are

   (1) congruent but not similar
   (2) similar but not congruent
   (3) both congruent and similar
   (4) neither congruent nor similar

Correct Answer: (2) similar but not congruent. Since a dilation of 3 will multiply each coordinate of the triangle by the number 3, the new figure will an enlargement of the original figure, but with the same proportions. Similar triangles have sides that are in proportion. Congruent triangles must have sides that have the exact same lengths. (*Similar Figures*)

5. The ages of five children in a family are 3, 3, 5, 8, and 18. Which statement is true for this group of data?

   (1) mode > mean
   (2) mean > median
   (3) median = mode
   (4) median > mean

Correct Answer: (2) mean > median. First, find the mean, median, and mode for this set of data. The mean requires you to add up the data and divide by the number of pieces of data. In this case, 3 + 3 + 5 + 8 + 18 = 37. The mean is 37 ÷ 5 = 7.4. The median requires you to place the data in order from least to greatest and find the middle number, in this case 5. The mode is the most common number in the set, namely 3. (*Statistics*)

6. On a map, 1 centimeter represents 40 kilometers. How many kilometers are represented by 8 centimeters?

   (1) 5
   (2) 48
   (3) 280
   (4) 320

Correct Answer: (4) 320. You can set up a proportion to relate centimeters to kilometers. $\frac{1}{40} = \frac{8}{x}$. Cross-multiplying results in an answer of 320 kilometers. (*Scale Drawing*)

7. If the area of a square garden is 48 square feet, what is the length, in feet, of one side of the garden?

   (1) $12\sqrt{2}$
   (2) $4\sqrt{3}$
   (3) $16\sqrt{3}$
   (4) $4\sqrt{6}$

Correct Answer: (2) $4\sqrt{3}$. The formula for the area of a square is $A = s^2$. In this case, $48 = s^2$. To solve for s, take the square root of both sides of the equation, resulting in $s = \sqrt{48}$. This is simplified to $\sqrt{16} \cdot \sqrt{3}$, or $4\sqrt{3}$. (*Area of Figures*)

8. M is the midpoint of AB. If the coordinates of A are $(-1,5)$ and the coordinates of M are $(3,3)$, what are the coordinates of B?

   (1) $(1,4)$
   (2) $(2,8)$
   (3) $(7,1)$
   (4) $(-5,7)$

Correct Answer: (3) $(7,1)$. A midpoint is the same distance from each endpoint. The x-coordinate of the midpoint, 3, is 4 units away from -1, so the other endpoint should have an x-coordinate 4 units away from 3 on the other side, namely 7. The y-coordinate of the midpoint, 3, is 2 units away from 5, so the other endpoint should have a y-coordinate 2 units away from 5 on the other side, namely 1. (*Coordinate Geometry*).

9. If the circumference of a circle is doubled, the diameter of the circle

    (1) remains the same
    (2) increases by 2
    (3) is multiplied by 4
    (4) is doubled

Correct Answer: (4) is doubled. For this question, it may be useful to plug in some numbers into the circumference formula, $C = \pi d$, to see how values may change. For example, if $C = 12\pi$, the diameter of the circle is 12. If you double this circumference, $2(12\pi)$, the new circumference is 24π, making its diameter 24. 24 is double the original diameter. (*Circumference of Circles*)

Open-Ended Questions

10. Seth bought a used car that had been driven 20,000 miles. After he owned the car for 2 years, the total mileage of the car was 49,400. Find the average number of miles he drove *each month* during those 2 years.

Correct Answer: 1,225. First find the number of miles Seth drove in the 2-year period. Subtract 20,000 from 49,400 to get 29,400 miles. There are 24 months in 2 years so divide the total miles Seth drove by 24 to get the average he drove each month. The answer is 1,225 miles. *(Units of Measurement)*

11. Tina's preschool has a set of cardboard building blocks, each of which measures 9 inches by 9 inches by 4 inches. How many of these blocks will Tina need to build a wall 4 inches thick, 3 feet high, and 12 feet long?

Correct Answer: 64. Using the formula $V = LWH$, you find that the volume of each original block is $9 \times 9 \times 4$ or 324 cubic inches. The structure that Tina wants to build has a volume of $4 \times 36 \times 144 = 20736$ cubic inches (take care to convert feet to inches). Then divide 20736 by 324 to determine that 64 of Tina's blocks are needed. (*Volume of Solids*)

12. A fish tank with a rectangular base has a volume of 3,360 cubic inches. The length and width of the tank are 14 inches and 12 inches, respectively. Find the height, in inches, of the tank.

Correct Answer: 20. Using the formula $V = LWH$, you can plug in the values that you are given and solve for the height. $3360 = 14 \times 12 \times H$. Therefore, $3360 = 168H$. Dividing both sides by 168 results in a height of 20 inches. (*Volume of Solids*)

13. An image of a building in a photograph is 6 centimeters wide and 11 centimeters tall. If the image is similar to the actual building and the actual building is 174 meters wide, how tall is the actual building, in meters?

Correct Answer: 319. Since the figures are similar, set up a proportion to relate their sides. $6/11 = 174/x$. After cross-multiplying, you get $1914 = 6x$. Dividing both sides by 6 results in an answer of 319. (*Similar Figures*)

Statistics and Probability

Multiple-Choice Questions

1. The weights of all the students in grade 9 are arranged from least to greatest. Which statistical measure separates the top half of this set of data from the bottom half?

   (1) mean
   (2) mode
   (3) median
   (4) average

Correct Answer: (3) median. The median of a set of data is the number in the middle when the set is arranged in order from least to greatest. Mean is another word for average so 1 and 4 are the same. Mode is the number in the set that occurs most often. *(Organization and Display of Data)*

2. The accompanying box-and-whisker plot represents the scores earned on a science test.

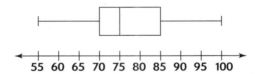

   What is the median score?

   (1) 70
   (2) 75
   (3) 77
   (4) 85

Correct Answer: (2) 75. The median is the number corresponding to the line segment inside the box of the box-and-whiskers plot. *(Organization and Display of Data)*

3. A deli has five types of meat, two types of cheese, and three types of bread. How many different sandwiches, consisting of one type of meat, one type of cheese, and one type of bread, does the deli serve?

(1) 10

(2) 25

(3) 30

(4) 75

Correct Answer: (3) 30. Using the product rule, you multiply the number of options, $5 \times 2 \times 3 = 30$. *(Probability)*

4. Jorge made the accompanying stem-and-leaf plot of the weights, in pounds, of each member of the wrestling team he was coaching.

Stem	Leaf						
10	9						
11							
12	3	8					
13	2	4	4	6	8		
14	1	3	5	5	9		
15	2	3	7	7	9		
16	1	3	7	8	8	8	9
17	3	8					

Key: 16 | 1 = 161

What is the mode of the weights?

(1) 145

(2) 150

(3) 152

(4) 168

Correct Answer: (4) 168. Mode is the number in the data set that occurs most often. Since the 8 appears as a leaf for 16 three times, that means there are three entries that are 168. When you analyze the stem-and-leaf plot, the number 168 appears the most often. *(Analysis of Data)*

5. Seth tossed a fair coin five times and got five heads. The probability that the next toss will be a tail is

(1) 0

(2) $\frac{1}{6}$

(3) $\frac{5}{6}$

(4) $\frac{1}{2}$

Correct Answer: (4) $\frac{1}{2}$. It does not matter that Seth tossed this coin five previous times. The probability for each toss is independent, meaning that one toss does not influence any of the other tosses. Therefore, there are still two possible outcomes, one of which is tails. This makes the probability $\frac{1}{2}$. *(Probability)*

6. The accompanying histogram shows the heights of the students in Kyra's health class.

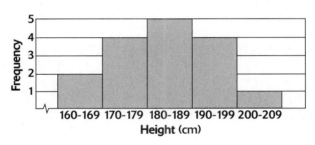

What is the total number of students in this class?

(1) 5

(2) 15

(3) 16

(4) 209

Correct Answer: (3) 16. Adding up the frequency in each column would give you: 2 + 4 + 5 + 4 + 1 = 16. *(Analysis of Data)*

7. How many different outfits consisting of a hat, a pair of slacks, and a sweater can be made from two hats, three pairs of slacks, and four sweaters?

(1) 9

(2) 12

(3) 24

(4) 29

Correct Answer: (3) 24. (2)(3)(4) = 24. *(Probability)*

8. Robin has eight blouses, six skirts, and five scarves. Which expression can be used to calculate the number of different outfits she can choose, if an outfit consists of a blouse, a skirt, and a scarf?

(1) $8 + 6 + 5$
(2) $8 \cdot 6 \cdot 5$
(3) $8!\ 6!\ 5!$
(4) $_{19}C_3$

Correct Answer: (2) $8 \cdot 6 \cdot 5$. Robin can match every one of the eight blouses with a different skirt, making $8 \cdot 6$ outfits consisting of a blouse and a skirt. She can match each of these outfits with any of the five different scarves. This yields $8 \cdot 6 \cdot 5$ different outfits consisting of a blouse, a skirt, and a scarf. *(Analysis of Data)*

9. How many different three-member teams can be selected from a group of seven students?

(1) 1
(2) 35
(3) 210
(4) 5,040

Correct Answer: (2) 35. This is a permutation because the order of the teams does not matter, so the formula would be $_nP_r$ where n is the total number of possibilities and r is the number considered at one time. In this case, $n = 7$, and $r = 3$ and $_7P_3$ is 210. *(Probability)*

10. Which value is equivalent to $_3P_3$?

(1) 1
(2) 9
(3) 3!
(4) 27

Correct Answer: (3) 3! The notation $_nP_r$ means "the permutation of n things, taken r at a time." You should list out r factors counting down from n. In this case $_3P_3$ means $3(3 - 1)(3 - 2)$ or $3 \cdot 2 \cdot 1 = 6$. This is the same value as choice (3) since $3! = 3 \cdot 2 \cdot 1 = 6$. *(Probability)*

11. Which inequality represents the probability, x, of any event happening?

(1) $x \geq 0$
(2) $0 < x < 1$
(3) $x < 1$
(4) $0 \leq x \leq 1$

Correct Answer: (4) $0 \leq x \leq 1$. The probability of an event that is certain to occur is 1. The probability of an event that cannot occur is 0. The probability of any other events is between 0 and 1. *(Probability)*

12. A student council has seven officers, of which five are girls and two are boys. If two officers are chosen at random to attend a meeting with the principal, what is the probability that the first officer is a girl and the second is a boy?

(1) $\frac{10}{42}$

(2) $\frac{2}{7}$

(3) $\frac{7}{14}$

(4) $\frac{7}{13}$

Correct Answer: (1) $\frac{10}{42}$. Since the events are consecutive, their probabilities would be multiplied. The probability of choosing a girl first is $\frac{5}{7}$, and the probability of choosing a boy next is $\frac{2}{6}$. $\frac{5}{7} \times \frac{2}{6} = \frac{10}{42}$. *(Probability)*

13. Mary chooses an integer at random from 1 to 6. What is the probability that the integer she chooses is a prime number?

(1) $\frac{5}{6}$

(2) $\frac{3}{6}$

(3) $\frac{2}{6}$

(4) $\frac{4}{6}$

Correct Answer: (2) $\frac{3}{6}$. A prime number is a number with only two distinct factors, itself and 1. There are 3 prime numbers from 1 to 6: 2, 3, and 5. *(Probability)*

14. If the Math Olympiad Club consists of 18 students, how many different teams of 4 students can be formed for competitions?

(1) 66

(2) 72

(3) 3,060

(4) 73,440

Correct Answer: (3) 3,060. Since you're looking to form groups or teams where order does not matter, you must use the combination notation $_nC_r$, where n is the number of items and r is the size of the group. $_{18}C_4 = (_{18}P_4)/(4!) = 3,060$. *(Probability)*

15. In a school building, there are 10 doors that can be used to enter the building and 8 stairways to the second floor. How many different routes are there from outside the building to a class on the second floor?

(1) 1
(2) 10
(3) 18
(4) 80

Correct Answer: (4) 80. For every door, there are 8 different possible stairways to take; since there are 10 doors to the building, $10(8) = 80$. *(Analysis of Data)*

16. Rosario and Enrique are in the same mathematics class. On the first five tests, Rosario received scores of 78, 77, 64, 86, and 70. Enrique received scores of 90, 61, 79, 73, and 87. How much higher was Enrique's average than Rosario's average?

(1) 15 points
(2) 2 points
(3) 3 points
(4) 4 points

Correct Answer: (3) 3 points. Rosario's average = $\dfrac{78 + 77 + 64 + 86 + 70}{5} = 75$. Enrico's average = $\dfrac{90 + 61 + 79 + 73 + 87}{5} = 78$. Erico's average is 3 points higher than Rosario's average. *(Analysis of Data)*

17. In a game, each player receives 5 cards from a deck of 52 different cards. How many different groupings of cards are possible in this game?

(1) $_{52}P_5$
(2) $_{52}C_5$
(3) $\dfrac{52!}{5!}$
(4) $5!$

Correct Answer: (2) $_{52}C_5$. *(Probability)*

18. Melissa's test scores are 75, 83, and 75. Which statement is true about this set of data?

   (1) mean < mode
   (2) mode < median
   (3) mode = median
   (4) mean = median

Correct Answer: (3) mode = median. The mode is the number that appears most often, in this case, 75. The median is the number in the middle when the data is ordered, in this case, 75. The mean is the average of all the numbers, $\frac{75 + 75 + 83}{3} = 77.\overline{6}$. The median and mode are equal. *(Analysis of Data)*

19. Five people have volunteered to work on an awards dinner at Madison High School. How many different committees of four can be formed from the five people?

   (1) 1
   (2) 5
   (3) 10
   (4) 20

Correct Answer: (2) 5. The order in which the people are picked doesn't matter so you use combinations: $_5C_4 = 5$. *(Probability)*

20. The accompanying graph shows the high temperatures in Elmira, New York, for a 5-day period in January.

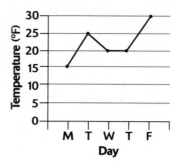

Which statement describes the data?

(1) median = mode
(2) median = mean
(3) mean < mode
(4) mean = mode

Correct Answer: (1) median = mode. The temperatures for the 5-day period are 15, 25, 20, 20, 30. The mode is 20 because it's the number that occurs most often. The mean is the average $\frac{15 + 25 + 20 + 20 + 30}{5} = 22$. The median is 20 because it is the number in the middle when the data is arranged in order. The mode and median are both 20. *(Analysis of Data)*

21. The expression $_9C_2$ is equivalent to

(1) $_9P_2$
(2) $_9P_7$
(3) $_9C_7$
(4) $\frac{9!}{2!}$

Correct Answer: (3) $_9C_7$. Plug the choices into a calculator and choice (3) is the same as the expression given. *(Probability)*

22. The accompanying Venn diagram shows the results of a survey asking 100 people if they get news by reading newspapers or by watching television.

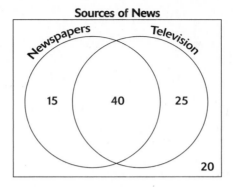

Sources of News

What is the probability that a person selected at random from this survey does *not* claim television as a source of getting the news?

(1) $\frac{15}{100}$

(2) $\frac{35}{100}$

(3) $\frac{55}{100}$

(4) $\frac{75}{100}$

Correct Answer: (2) $\frac{35}{100}$. Since 65 out of 100 people get the news by watching television, 35 out of 100 people get the news by not watching television. *(Probability)*

23. The school cafeteria offers five sandwich choices, four desserts, and three beverages. How many different meals consisting of one sandwich, one dessert, and one beverage can be ordered?

(1) 1

(2) 12

(3) 3

(4) 60

Correct Answer: (4) 60. $5 \cdot 4 \cdot 3 = 60$. *(Probability)*

24. Julia has four different flags that she wants to hang on the wall of her room. How many different ways can the flags be arranged in a row?

(1) 1

(2) 10

(3) 16

(4) 24

Correct Answer: (4) 24. There are 4 flags, all of which need to be arranged, $_4P_4 = 24$. *(Probability)*

25. The Edison Lightbulb Company tests 5% of their daily production of lightbulbs. If 500 bulbs were tested on Tuesday, what was the total number of bulbs produced that day?

(1) 25

(2) 1,000

(3) 10,000

(4) 100,000

Correct Answer: (3) 10,000. Let x = the total number of bulbs produced that day. Then, 5% $x = 500 \rightarrow$ $0.05x = 500$. Divide both sides by 0.05: $x = 10,000$. *(Analysis of Data)*

26. The probability that the Cubs win their first game is $\frac{1}{3}$. The probability that the Cubs win their second game is $\frac{3}{7}$. What is the probability that the Cubs win both games?

(1) $\frac{16}{21}$

(2) $\frac{1}{7}$

(3) $\frac{6}{7}$

(4) $\frac{2}{5}$

Correct Answer: (2) $\frac{1}{7}$. Multiply the probability of winning the first game by the probability of winning the second game. These games are considered consecutive events so you multiply their probabilities. *(Probability)*

27. Seventy-eight students participate in one or more of three sports: baseball, tennis, and golf. Four students participate in all three sports; five play both baseball and golf, only; two play both tennis and golf, only; and three play both baseball and tennis, only. If seven students play only tennis and one plays only golf, what is the total number of students who play only baseball?

(1) 12

(2) 44

(3) 56

(4) 60

Correct Answer: (3) 56.

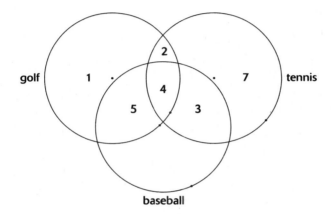

Number of students playing only baseball = 78 − 4 − 5 − 2 − 3 − 7 − 1 = 56. *(Probability)*

28. Selena and Tracey play on a softball team. Selena has 8 hits out of 20 times at bat, and Tracey has 6 hits out of 16 times at bat. Based on their past performance, what is the probability that both girls will get a hit next time at bat?

(1) 1

(2) $\frac{14}{36}$

(3) $\frac{31}{40}$

(4) $\frac{48}{320}$

Correct Answer: (4) $\frac{48}{320}$. Since these are independent events, that is the girls' performance does not affect the other, P(Selena has a hit and Tracey has a hit) = P(Selena has a hit) · P(Tracy has a hit) = $\frac{8}{20} \cdot \frac{6}{16} = \frac{48}{320}$. *(Probability)*

29. A committee of five members is to be randomly selected from a group of nine freshmen and seven sophomores. Which expression represents the number of different committees of three freshmen and two sophomores that can be chosen?

(1) $_9C_3 + {_7}C_2$

(2) $_9C_3 \cdot {_7}C_2$

(3) $_{16}C_3 \cdot {_{16}}C_2$

(4) $_9P_3 + {_7}P_2$

Correct Answer: (2) $_9C_3 \cdot {_7}C_2$. The number of combinations of 3 freshmen out of 9 freshmen is $_9C_3.$ The number of combinations of 2 sophomores out of 7 sophomores is $_7C_2.$ So, the total number of different committees of 3 freshmen and 2 sophomores is $_9C_3 \cdot {_7}C_2$.

30. In the next Olympics, the United States can enter four athletes in the diving competition. How many different teams of four divers can be selected from a group of nine divers?

(1) 36

(2) 126

(3) 3,024

(4) 6,561

Correct Answer: (2) 126. You want to rearrange 4 out of 9 athletes, $_9P_4 = 126$. *(Probability)*

150

Open-Ended Questions

31. The following set of data represents the scores on a mathematics quiz:

58, 79, 81, 99, 68, 92, 76, 84, 53, 57,

81, 91, 77, 50, 65, 57, 51, 72, 84, 89

Complete the frequency table that follows and draw a label a frequency histogram of these scores.

Mathematics Quiz Scores

Interval	Tally	Frequency
50-59		
60-69		
70-79		
80-89		
90-99		

Correct Answer:

Mathematics Quiz Scores

Interval	Tally	Frequency
50-59	₩₩ I	6
60-69	II	2
70-79	IIII	4
80-89	₩₩	5
90-99	III	3

There are 6 scores between 50 and 59: 58, 53, 57, 50, 57, and 51; hence, the frequency for this interval is 6. There are 2 scores between 60 and 69: 68 and 65; hence, the frequency for this interval is 2. There are 4 scores between 70 and 79: 79, 76, 77, and 72; hence, the frequency for this interval is 4. There are 5 scores between 80 and 89: 81, 84, 81, 84, and 89; hence, the frequency for this interval is 5. There are 3 scores between 90 and 99: 99, 92, and 91; hence, the frequency of this interval is 3. *(Statistics)*

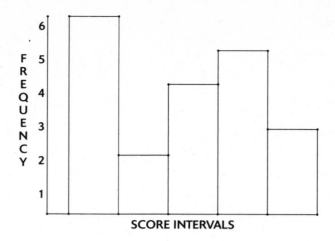

32. In Clark Middle School, there are 60 students in seventh grade. If 25 of these students take art only, 18 take music only, and 9 do not take either art or music, how many take both art and music?

Correct Answer: 8 students take both art and music. $60 - (25 + 18 + 9) = 8$. *(Analysis of Data)*

33. TOP Electronics is a small business with five employees. The mean (average) weekly salary for the five employees is $360. If the weekly salaries of four of the employees are $340, $340, $345, and $425, what is the salary of the fifth employee?

Correct Answer: $350. Let x = the salary of the fifth employee. $\dfrac{340 + 340 + 345 + 425 + x}{5} = 360$.

Multiply both sides by 5: $340 + 340 + 345 + 425 + x = 1,800 \rightarrow 1450 + x = 1,800$. Subtract 14.50 from both sides: $x = \$350$. *(Predictions from Data)*

34. Debbie goes to a diner famous for its express lunch menu. The menu has five appetizers, three soups, seven entrees, six vegetables, and four desserts. How many different meals consisting of either an appetizer *or* a soup, one entree, one vegetable, and one dessert can Debbie order?

Correct Answer: Debbie can order 1,344 different meals. $8 \cdot 7 \cdot 6 \cdot 4 = 1,344$. *(Predictions from Data)*

35. On the first six tests in her social studies course, Jerelyn's scores were 92, 78, 86, 92, 95, and 91. Determine the median and the mode of her scores. If Jerelyn took a seventh test and raised the mean of her scores *exactly* 1 point, what was her score on the seventh test?

Correct Answer: Median = 91.5, Mode = 92, 7th score = 96. Since there is an even number of scores, the median is the average of the two middle scores when the scores are arranged in order: $\dfrac{91 + 92}{2} = 91.5$; the mode is the number that occurs most often.

Mean = $\dfrac{92 + 78 + 86 + 92 + 95 + 91}{6} = 89$. Let the score on the 7th test equal x. Then,

$90 = \dfrac{92 + 78 + 86 + 92 + 95 + 91 + x}{7}$. Cross-multiply: $630 = 534 + x$. Subtract 534 from both sides:

$x = 96$. *(Analysis of Data)*

36. In Jackson County, Wyoming, license plates are made with two letters (*A* through *Z*) followed by three digits (0 through 9). The plates are made according to the following restrictions:

- The first letter must be *J* or *W*, and the second letter can be any of the 26 letters in the alphabet.
- No digit can be repeated.

How many different license plates can be made with these restrictions?

Correct Answer: There are 37,440 different license plates possible. There are **2** choices for the first letter, *J* or *W*. There are **26** choices for the second letter, any of the 26 letters of the alphabet. There are **10** choices for the first digit, any digit from 0 to 9; there are **9** choices for the second digit (since no digits can be repeated); and **8** choices for the third digit. The total number of possible license plates is $2(26)(10)(9)(8) = 37,440$. *(Probability)*

37. The accompanying table shows the weights, in pounds, for the students in an algebra class. Using the data, complete the cumulative frequency table that follows and construct a cumulative frequency histogram on the grid on the next page.

Interval	Frequency	Cumulative Frequency
91-100	6	
101-110	3	
111-120	0	
121-130	3	
131-140	0	
141-150	2	
151-160	2	

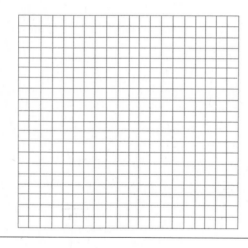

Correct Answer:

Interval	Frequency	Cumulative Frequency
91-100	6	6
101-110	3	9
111-120	0	9
121-130	3	12
131-140	0	12
141-150	2	14
151-160	2	16

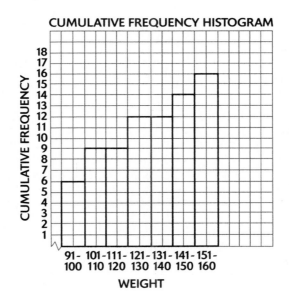

(Organization and Display of Data)

38. The accompanying diagram shows a square dartboard. The side of the dartboard measures 30 inches. The square shaded region at the center has a side that measures 10 inches. If darts thrown at the board are equally likely to land anywhere on the board, what is the theoretical probability that a dart does *not* land in the shaded region?

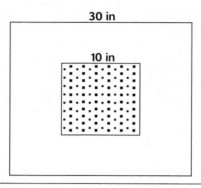

30 in

10 in

Correct Answer: $\frac{800}{900}$. $\text{Area}_{\text{outer square}} = 30^2 = 900$ square inches. $\text{Area}_{\text{inner square}} = 10^2 = 100$ square inches.

The probability that the dart does *not* land in the shaded region is $\frac{900 - 100}{900} = \frac{800}{900}$. *(Probability)*

39. The senior class at South High School consists of 250 students. Of these students, 130 have brown hair, 160 have brown eyes, and 90 have both brown hair and brown eyes. How many members of the senior class have *neither* brown hair *nor* brown eyes?

Correct Answer: 50 members of the senior class have neither brown hair nor brown eyes. *(Organization and Display of Data)*

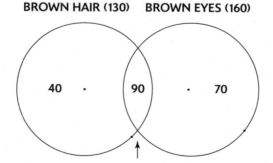

BROWN HAIR (130) BROWN EYES (160)

40 · 90 · 70

Number of students with brown hair and/or brown eyes: $40 + 90 + 70 = 200$.

Number of students with neither brown hair nor brown eyes: $250 - 200 = 50$.

40. Kimberly has three pair of pants: one black, one red, and one tan. She also has four shirts: one pink, one white, one yellow, and one green.

Draw a tree diagram or list the sample space showing all possible outfits that she could wear, if an outfit consists of one pair of pants and one shirt.

How many different outfits can Kimberly wear?

Correct Answer:

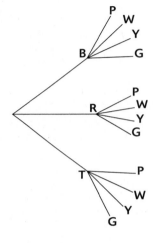

Tree diagram

(B,P) (R,P) (T,P)
(B,W) (R,W) (T,W)
(B,Y) (R,Y) (T,Y)
(B,G) (R,G) (T,G)

Sample space

(Analysis of Data)

41. Construct a stem-and-leaf plot listing the scores below in order from lowest to highest.

15, 25, 28, 32, 39, 40, 43, 26, 50, 75, 65, 19, 55, 72, 50

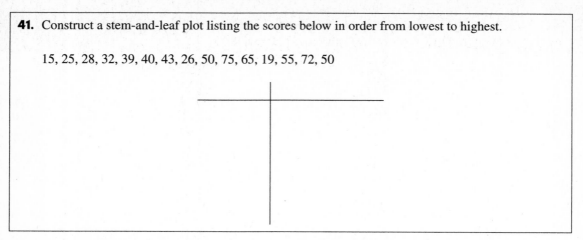

Correct Answer: The answer is the plot. To correctly plot the numbers, label the left column "tens" and the right column "ones." Write all the numbers appearing in the tens place in the left column once, and then write the ones part in the right column. If there are two 15s, then the one would appear once and there would be two 5s. Lastly, you must create a key such as 1|5 = 15. *(Organization and Display of Data)*

Self-Evaluation Test
with Answer Explanations

1	①	②	③	④
2	①	②	③	④
3	①	②	③	④
4	①	②	③	④
5	①	②	③	④
6	①	②	③	④
7	①	②	③	④
8	①	②	③	④
9	①	②	③	④
10	①	②	③	④
11	①	②	③	④
12	①	②	③	④
13	①	②	③	④
14	①	②	③	④
15	①	②	③	④
16	①	②	③	④
17	①	②	③	④
18	①	②	③	④
19	①	②	③	④
20	①	②	③	④
21	①	②	③	④
22	①	②	③	④
23	①	②	③	④
24	①	②	③	④
25	①	②	③	④
26	①	②	③	④
27	①	②	③	④
28	①	②	③	④
29	①	②	③	④
30	①	②	③	④

Reference Sheet

The Regents Examination in Integrated Algebra will include a reference sheet containing the formulas specified here:

Trigonometric Ratios	$\sin A = \dfrac{opposite}{hypotenuse}$
	$\cos A = \dfrac{adjacent}{hypotenuse}$
	$\tan A = \dfrac{opposite}{hypotenuse}$

| Area | trapezoid | $A = \frac{1}{2}h(b_1 + b_2)$ |

| Volume | cylinder | $V = \pi r^2 h$ |

| Surface Area | rectangular prism | $SA = 2lw + 2hw + 2lh$ |
| | cylinder | $SA = 2\pi r^2 + 2\pi rh$ |

| Formulas for Coordinate Geometry | $m = \dfrac{\Delta y}{\Delta x} = \dfrac{y_2 - y_1}{x_2 - x_1}$ |
| | $M = \left(\dfrac{x_1 + x_2}{2}, \dfrac{y_1 + y_2}{2} \right)$ |

Multiple-Choice Questions (Part I)

1. The accompanying graph shows the amount of water left in Rover's water dish over a period of time.

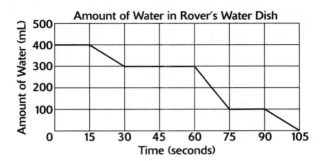

How long did Rover wait from the end of his first drink to the start of his second drink of water?

(1) 10 sec

(2) 30 sec

(3) 60 sec

(4) 75 sec

2. In Ms. Wright's English class, 16 students are in band, 7 students play sports, 3 students participate in both activities, and 9 students are not in band and do not play sports. How many students are in Ms. Wright's English class?

(1) 10

(2) 26

(3) 29

(4) 35

3. Sal keeps quarters, nickels, and dimes in his change jar. He has a total of 52 coins. He has 3 more quarters than dimes and 5 fewer nickels than dimes. How many dimes does Sal have?

(1) 13

(2) 18

(3) 20

(4) 21

4. Which equation illustrates the distributive property of multiplication over addition?

(1) $6(3a + 4b) = 18a + 4b$

(2) $6(3a + 4b) = 18a + 24b$

(3) $6(3a + 4b) = (3a + 4b)6$

(4) $6(3a + 4b) = 6(4b + 3a)$

5. What is the *y*-intercept of the graph of the line whose equation is $y = -\frac{2}{5}x + 4$?

(1) $-\frac{5}{2}$

(2) $-\frac{2}{5}$

(3) 0

(4) 4

6. Which point on the accompanying number line best represents the position of $\sqrt{5}$?

(1) *A*

(2) *B*

(3) *C*

(4) *D*

7. The ratio of two supplementary angles is 2:7. What is the measure of the *smaller* angle?

(1) 10°

(2) 14°

(3) 20°

(4) 40°

8. The faces of a cube are numbered from 1 to 6. What is the probability of *not* rolling a 5 on a single toss of this cube?

(1) $\frac{1}{6}$

(2) $\frac{5}{6}$

(3) $\frac{1}{5}$

(4) $\frac{4}{5}$

9. What is the value of *p* in the equation $2(3p - 4) = 10$?

(1) 1

(2) $2\frac{1}{3}$

(3) 3

(4) $\frac{1}{3}$

10. The formula for potential energy is $P = mgh$, where P is potential energy, m is mass, g is gravity, and h is height. Which expression can be used to represent g?

    (1) $P - m - h$

    (2) $P - mh$

    (3) $\dfrac{P}{m} - h$

    (4) $\dfrac{P}{mh}$

11. The expression $8^{-4} \cdot 8^6$ is equivalent to

    (1) 8^{-24}

    (2) 8^{-2}

    (3) 8^2

    (4) 8^{10}

12. Which statement describes the graph of $x = 4$?

    (1) It passes through the point $(0, 4)$.

    (2) It has a slope of 4.

    (3) It is parallel to the y-axis.

    (4) It is parallel to the x-axis.

13. The statement "x is divisible by 5 or x is divisible by 4" is false when x equals

    (1) 10

    (2) 16

    (3) 20

    (4) 27

14. The sum of Scott's age and Greg's age is 33 years. If Greg's age is represented by g, Scott's age is represented by

    (1) $33 - g$

    (2) $g - 33$

    (3) $g + 33$

    (4) $33g$

15. The accompanying diagram shows the graphs of a linear equation and a quadratic equation.

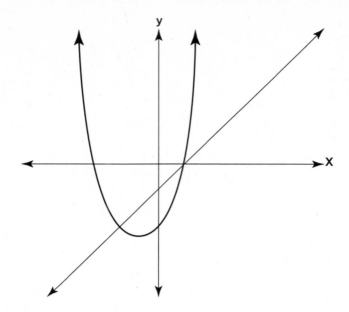

How many solutions are there to this system of equations?

(1) 1
(2) 2
(3) 3
(4) 0

16. The angle of elevation from a point 25 feet from the base of a tree on level ground to the top of the tree is 30°. Which equation can be used to find the height of the tree?

(1) $\tan 30° = \frac{x}{25}$

(2) $\cos 30° = \frac{x}{25}$

(3) $\sin 30° = \frac{x}{25}$

(4) $30^2 + 25^2 = x^2$

17. Stan was trying to guess Melanie's age. She told him her age was an even number and a multiple of three. What could be Melanie's age?

(1) 10
(2) 12
(3) 15
(4) 16

18. The midpoint of $\overline{AB}$ is (–1,5), and the coordinates of point A are (–3,2). What are the coordinates of point B?

(1) (1,8)

(2) (1,10)

(3) (0,7)

(4) (–5,8)

19. The expression $(x^2 – 5x – 2) – (–6x^2 – 7x – 3)$ is equivalent to

(1) $7x^2 – 12x – 5$

(2) $7x^2 – 2x + 1$

(3) $7x^2 + 2x + 1$

(4) $7x^2 + 2x – 5$

20. What is the value of n in the equation $0.6(n + 10) = 3.6$?

(1) –0.4

(2) 5

(3) –4

(4) 4

21. Which is an equation of the line of symmetry for the parabola in the accompanying diagram?

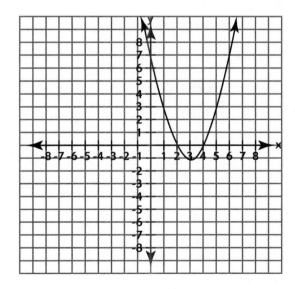

(1) $x = 2$

(2) $x = 4$

(3) $x = 3$

(4) $y = 3$

22. The formula for the volume of a right circular cylinder is $V = \pi r^2 h$. The value of h can be expressed as

(1) $\dfrac{V}{\pi} r^2$

(2) $\dfrac{V}{\pi r^2}$

(3) $\dfrac{\pi r^2}{V}$

(4) $V - \pi r^2$

23. What is the solution set of the equation $\dfrac{x}{5} + \dfrac{x}{2} = 14$?

(1) {4}
(2) {10}
(3) {20}
(4) {49}

24. Which statement about quadrilaterals is true?

(1) All quadrilaterals have four right angles.
(2) All quadrilaterals have equal sides.
(3) All quadrilaterals have four sides.
(4) All quadrilaterals are parallelograms.

25. The image of point A after a dilation of 3 is (6, 15). What was the original location of point A?

(1) (2,5)
(2) (3,12)
(3) (9,18)
(4) (18,45)

26. In the accompanying diagram, lines *a* and *b* are parallel, and *c* and *d* are transversals.

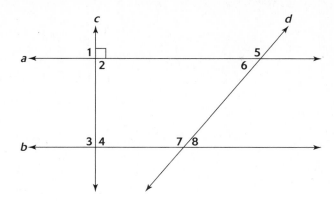

Which angle is congruent to angle 8?

(1) 6

(2) 5

(3) 3

(4) 4

27. What is a common factor of $x^2 - 9$ and $x^2 - 5x + 6$?

(1) $x + 3$

(2) $x - 3$

(3) $x - 2$

(4) x^2

28. A planned building was going to be 100 feet long, 75 feet deep, and 30 feet high. The owner decides to increase the volume of the building by 10% without changing the dimensions of the depth and height. What will be the new length of this building?

(1) 106 ft

(2) 108 ft

(3) 110 ft

(4) 112 ft

29. The test scores for 10 students in Ms. Sampson's homeroom were 61, 67, 81, 83, 87, 88, 89, 90, 98, and 100. Which frequency table is accurate for this set of data?

(1)

Interval	Frequency
61-70	2
71-80	2
81-90	7
91-100	10

(2)

Interval	Frequency
61-70	2
71-80	2
81-90	8
91-100	10

(3)

Interval	Frequency
61-70	2
71-80	0
81-90	8
91-100	10

(4)

Interval	Frequency
61-70	2
71-80	0
81-90	6
91-100	2

30. If $a > 0$, then $\sqrt{9a^2 + 16a^2}$ equals

(1) $\sqrt{7a}$

(2) $5\sqrt{a}$

(3) $5a$

(4) $7a$

Open-Ended Questions (Parts II–IV)

31. As shown in the accompanying diagram, a ladder is leaning against a vertical wall, making an angle of 70° with the ground and reaching a height of 10.39 feet on the wall.

Find, to the nearest foot, the length of the ladder.

Find, to the nearest foot, the distance from the base of the ladder to the wall.

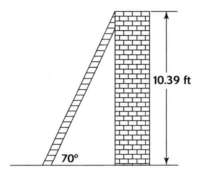

10.39 ft

70°

32. An algebra class of 21 students must send 5 students to meet with the principal. How many different groups of 5 students could be formed from this class?

33. Fran's favorite photograph has a length of 6 inches and a width of 4 inches. She wants to have it made into a poster with dimensions that are similar to those of the photograph. She determined that the poster should have a length of 24 inches. How many inches wide will the poster be?

34. The perimeter of a square is 56. Express the length of a diagonal of the square in simplest radical form.

35. The Eye Surgery Institute just purchased a new laser machine for $500,000 to use during eye surgery. The Institute must pay the inventor $550 each time the machine is used. If the Institute charges $2,000 for each laser surgery, what is the *minimum* number of surgeries that must be performed in order for the Institute to make a profit?

36. Sara's test scores in mathematics were 64, 80, 88, 78, 60, 92, 84, 76, 86, 78, 72, and 90. Determine the mean, the median, and the mode of Sara's test scores.

37. Solve the following system of equations algebraically or graphically. The use of the accompanying grid is optional.

$x^2 + y^2 = 25$

$3y - 4x = 0$

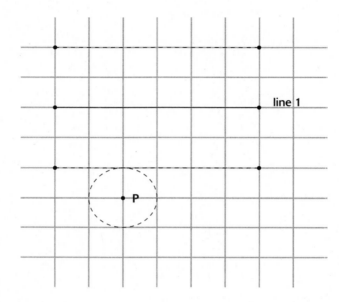

38. Tom throws a ball into the air. The ball travels on a parabolic path represented by the equation $h = -8t^2 + 40t$, where h is the height, in feet, and t is the time, in seconds.

    a. On the accompanying set of axes, graph the equation from $t = 0$ to $t = 5$ seconds, including all integral values of t from 0 to 5.

    b. What is the value of t at which h has its greatest value?

39. There are 30 students on a school bus. Of these students, 24 either play in the school band or sing in the chorus. Six of the students play in the school band but do not sing in the chorus. Fourteen of the students sing in the chorus and also play in the school band. How many students on the school bus sing in the chorus but do *not* play in the school band?

Answer Key

1. (2)	**11.** (3)	**21.** (3)
2. (3)	**12.** (3)	**22.** (2)
3. (2)	**13.** (4)	**23.** (3)
4. (2)	**14.** (1)	**24.** (3)
5. (4)	**15.** (2)	**25.** (1)
6. (3)	**16.** (1)	**26.** (1)
7. (4)	**17.** (2)	**27.** (2)
8. (2)	**18.** (1)	**28.** (3)
9. (3)	**19.** (3)	**29.** (4)
10. (4)	**20.** (3)	**30.** (3)

Answers and Explanations

1. **Correct Answer: (2)** 30 sec. He took his first drink after 15 seconds and finished it at 30 seconds. He then waited 30 seconds until he took the next drink. 60 – 30 = 30 seconds. *(Patterns, Relations, and Functions)*

2. **Correct Answer: (3)** 29. First, the number of students in the band and sports must be added together to get 23. Second, you subtract the 3 in both to get 20 and then add to students not counted who were in neither to get 29. *(Analysis of Data)*

3. **Correct Answer: (2)** 18. Let x = the number of dimes, $x + 3$ = the number of quarters, $x – 5$ = the number of nickels. Since the total number of coins is 52, $x + (x+3) + (x – 5) = 52$. Combine like terms: $3x – 2 = 52$. Add 2 to both sides: $3x = 54$. Divide both sides by 3: $x = 18$ dimes. *(Equations and Inequalities)*

4. **Correct Answer: (2)** $6(3a + 4b) = 18a + 24b$. The distributive property of multiplication over addition states that the factor outside the parentheses must be multiplied by each term inside the parentheses. *(Number Systems)*

5. **Correct Answer: (4)** 4. The standard form of a line's equation is $y = mx + b$, where b is the y intercept. In this case, $b = 4$. *(Equations and Inequalities)*

6. **Correct Answer: (3)** C. Since $2^2 = 4$ and $3^2 = 9$, the $\sqrt{5}$ must be located between 2 and 3. C is the only point in this location. Alternately, your calculator evaluates $\sqrt{5}$ as approximately 2.236. C best approximates this value. *(Estimation)*

7. **Correct Answer: (4)** 40°. Let the smaller angle measure be represented by $2x$ and the larger angle measure be represented by $7x$. Then, $2x + 7x = 180° \rightarrow 9x = 180 \rightarrow x = 20 \rightarrow 2(x) = 2(20) = 40°$. *(Geometric Relationships)*

8. **Correct Answer: (2)** $\frac{5}{6}$. Not rolling a 5 means rolling a 1, 2, 3, 4, or 6. The probability of rolling any of these five numbers out of the 6 is $\frac{5}{6}$. *(Probability)*

9. **Correct Answer: (3)** 3. $2(3p – 4) = 10$. Distribute 2: $6p – 8 = 10$. Add 8 to both sides: $6p = 18$. Divide both sides by 6: $p = 3$. *(Equations and Inequalities)*

10. **Correct Answer: (4)** P/mh. In order to solve for g, you must isolate it. Since m, g, and h are all multiplied together, divide both sides by m and h. This gets g alone. *(Equations and Inequalities)*

11. **Correct Answer: (3)** 8^2. When multiplying expressions with equal bases, keep the base the same and add the powers. Hence, $8^{-4} \cdot 8^6 = 8^{-4+6} = 8^2$. *(Operations)*

12. **Correct Answer: (3)** It is parallel to the y-axis. The graph of $x = 4$ is a line containing all points with an x-coordinate of 4 such as (–2,4), (–1,4), (0,4), (1,4), (2,4), and so on. All these points lie on a vertical line. Every vertical line is parallel to the y-axis. *(Patterns, Relations, and Functions)*

13. **Correct Answer: (4)** 27. An "or" statement, otherwise known as a disjunction, is false when both parts of the statement are false. If one of the parts is true or both parts are true, then that makes the entire disjunction true. When 27 is plugged into "x is divisible by 5" for x, then that is false and when 27 is plugged into "x is divisible by 4" for x, which also is false, the entire disjunction is false. *(Informal Proofs)*

14. Correct Answer: (1) $33 - g$. If both of their ages add to 33 and you know that Greg's age is g, subtract g from 33 to get $33 - g$. For example, if you know that Greg is 20, then Scott's age must be $(33 - 20)$, which equals 13. *(Variables and Expressions)*

15. Correct Answer: (2) 2. The solution(s) to a system of equations occur at the point(s) where the two graphs intersect. There are two places where the quadratic equation and linear equation intersect. *(Coordinate Geometry)*

16. Correct Answer: (1) $\tan 30° = \frac{x}{25}$.

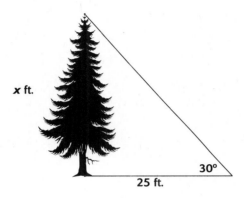

$\tan 30° = \dfrac{opposite\ side}{adjacent\ side} = \dfrac{x}{25}$. *(Trigonometry)*

17. Correct Answer: (2) 12. Choices 1 and 4 are both even, but not multiples of 3. Choice 3 is a multiple of 3, but not even. Choice 2 satisfies both parts. *(Patterns, Relations, and Functions)*

18. Correct Answer: (1) (1,8). The midpoint must be the same distance from point A as it is from point B. *(Coordinate Geometry)*

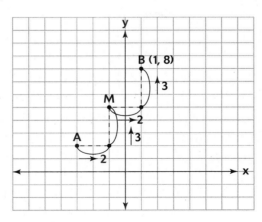

19. **Correct Answer: (3)** $7x^2 + 2x + 1$. Subtract each term in the second set of parentheses from its like term in the first set of parentheses. Do not change the exponents when adding or subtracting like terms. *(Variables and Expressions)*

20. **Correct Answer: (3)** –4. $0.6(n + 10) = 3.6$. Distribute 0.6: $0.6n + 6 = 3.6$. Subtract 6 from both sides: $0.6n = -2.4$. Divide both sides by 0.6: $n = -4$. *(Equations and Inequalities)*

21. **Correct Answer: (3)** $x = 3$. The axis of symmetry of a parabola is a vertical line that intersects the parabola's vertex. *(Patterns, Relations, and Functions)*

22. **Correct Answer: (2)** $\dfrac{V}{\pi r^2}$. To isolate h divide both sides by πr^2. *(Variables and Expressions)*

23. **Correct Answer: (3)** {20}. When adding fractions, you need to get a common denominator, which in this problem is 10. This gives you $\dfrac{7x}{10} = 14$; then multiplying both sides by 10, and dividing both sides by 7, gives you $x = 20$. *(Equations and Inequalities)*

24. **Correct Answer: (3)** All quadrilaterals have four sides. *(Shapes)*

25. **Correct Answer: (1)** (2,5). Dilations require you to multiply the dilation factor by each piece of the original coordinate. Here, the dilation is already complete, and you must undo it by division. $6 \div 3 = 2$ and $15 \div 3 = 5$. This gives you choice (1) (2,5). *(Transformational Geometry)*

26. **Correct Answer: (1)** 6. Choice 1 is an alternate interior angle with 8, while the others are all supplementary. *(Geometric Relationships)*

27. **Correct Answer: (2)** $x - 3$. $x^2 - 9 = (x + 3)(x - 3)$ and $x^2 - 5x + 6 = (x - 3)(x - 2)$. The common factor is $(x - 3)$. *(Variables and Expressions)*

28. **Correct Answer: (3)** 110 ft. First, calculate the original volume using $V = lwh = (100)(75)(30) = 225,000$. If you multiply 225,000 by 1.10, you receive the new increased volume of 247,500. You can set up a new equation $247,500 = L(75)(30)$ in order to solve for the new length. Choice (3) satisfies this equation. *(Tools and Methods)*

29. **Correct Answer: (4)**

Interval	Frequency
61-70	2
71-80	0
81-90	6
91-100	2

This is the only chart in which the frequencies add up to 10, that is, $2 + 0 + 6 + 2 = 10$. *(Organization and Display of Data)*

30. **Correct Answer: (3)** $5a$. $\sqrt{9a^2 + 16a^2}$. Combine like terms: $\sqrt{25a^2} = \sqrt{25}\sqrt{a^2} = 5a$. *(Variables and Expressions)*

31. **Correct Answer:** The length of the ladder is 11 feet. The distance from the base of the ladder to the wall is 4 feet.

Let x = length of ladder. Let y = the distance from the base of the ladder to the wall.

Then, $\sin(70°) = \frac{10.39}{x}$. Cross-multiply: $x \sin(70°) = 10.39$. Divide both sides by $\sin(70°)$: $x = 11$ feet.

Also, $\tan(70°) = \frac{10.39}{y}$. Cross-multiply: $y \tan(70°) = 10.39$. Divide both sides by $\tan(70°)$: $y = 4$ feet. *(Trigonometric Functions)*

32. **Correct Answer:** 20,349 groups. This is a combination problem ($_nC_r$) so do $_{21}C_5$. This equals 20,349. The key words in this problem are *different groups,* which usually indicates a combination problem. *(Probability)*

33. **Correct Answer:** 16 inches. This could be set up as the proportion: $\frac{6 \; inches}{4 \; inches} = \frac{24 \; inches}{x}$. Solving for x by cross-multiplying yields $x = 16$ inches. *(Operations)*

34. **Correct Answer:** $14\sqrt{2}$. Since all four sides of a square are equal in length, $56 \div 4$ results in a length of 14 for each side. Using the Pythagorean theorem, you say $14^2 + 14^2 = diagonal^2$. Then, $392 = diagonal^2$ and $\sqrt{392} = diagonal$. $\sqrt{392} = 14\sqrt{2}$. Alternately, recall the formula for the sides of a 45-45-90 triangle. *(Shapes)*

35. **Correct Answer:** 345. Since the Institute charges \$2,000 for each surgery but must pay \$550 for each surgery, the Institute really only profits \$1,450 each time a surgery is performed. The inequality $1450x > 500,000$ is used to find your solution. x results in 344.8275. However, you round this answer up to the next whole number, 345, to ensure a profit. *(Equations and Inequalities)*

36. **Correct Answer:** The mean is 79; the median is 79; the mode is 78.

On the calculator, to store the data in L_1, click STAT, pick choice 1:Edit). Find the mean and the median by pressing STAT, highlight CALC, pick 1:1-Var Stats, press ENTER, click 2nd, 1, ENTER. $\overline{x}$ is the mean, Med is the median. The mode is the number that appears most often; in this case it's 78. *(Analysis of Data)*

37. **Correct Answer:** (3,4) and (–3,–4). Algebraically: solve for y from the second equation: $y = \frac{4}{3}x$. Substitute this for y in the first equation and solve for x: $x^2 + \left(\frac{4}{3}x\right)^2 = 25 \rightarrow x^2 + \frac{16}{9}x^2 = 25 \rightarrow \frac{25}{9}x^2 = 25 \rightarrow x^2 = 9 \rightarrow x = 3$ or $x = -3$. Substitute these x-values into either equation to solve for y: $3y - 4(3) = 0 \rightarrow y = 4 \rightarrow$ one intersection point is (3,4).

$3y - 4(-3) = 0 \rightarrow y = -4 \rightarrow$ the other intersection point is $(-3,-4)$. Or, graph both the line and the circle and find their intersection points. *(Equations and Inequalities)*

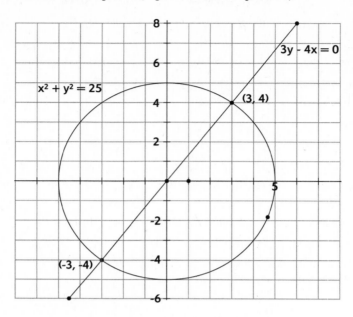

38. Correct Answer: *a.*

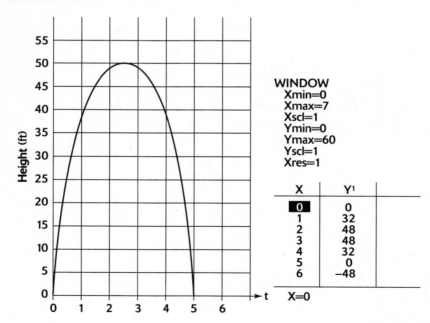

Correct Answer: *b*. The greatest value of *h* occurs at *t* = 2.5 seconds.

Algebraically, $t = -\dfrac{b}{2a} = -\dfrac{40}{2(-8)} = 2.5$.

Or, on your calculator, press 2nd, Trace, 4, 2 (for left bound), Enter, 3 (for right bound), Enter, Enter, Maximum: *x* = 2.5000000; *y* = 50. *(Patterns, Relations, and Functions)*

39. Correct Answer: 4. Use a Venn Diagram. Take the 24 students who are in band, chorus, or both and subtract out those who are in both, which is 14. This leaves 10 students who are in either band or chorus but not both. Subtract the 6 students who are in band only, which leaves 4 students who are only in chorus. *(Patterns, Relations, and Functions)*

Vocabulary for Integrated Algebra

Following are a list of terms that may be used in your Integrated Algebra Regents Examination or as part of your study of this course. Go through these terms and check off those you don't know. Then go back and study them. After you know the meaning of the terms, cross them off.

Problem Solving

algebraically

concept

conjecture

constraint

equivalent

formulate

generalization

graphically

multiple representations

numerically

parameter

pattern

relative efficiency

strategy

verbally

Reasoning and Proof

appropriate

approximation

argument

claim

conclusion

conjecture

counterexample

explain

inductive reasoning

logical argument

mathematical conjecture

proof

refute

systematic approach

validity

Venn diagram

verify

Communication

accuracy	formula
analyze	function
argument	graph
coherent	interpretation
communicate	mathematical visual
comprehension	rationale
conclusion	standard (mathematical) notation
conjecture	strategy
decoding	table
elicit	technical writing
equation	terminology
evaluate	valid
extend	

Connections

coherent whole	physical model
concept	procedure
connection	quantitative model
formulate	representation

Representation

angle of elevation	equation
array	function
chart	graph
compare	interpret
diagram	mathematical phenomena

organize

physical phenomena

profit

record

social phenomena

symbol

table

technology

translate

Number Sense and Operations

absolute value

algebraic problem

arithmetic operation

arrangements (permutations)

associative property

closure property

commutative property

counting techniques

decimal

denominator

discount

distributive property

exponential expression

expression

factorial

field

fraction

Fundamental Principle of Counting

group

identity property

inverse property

like/unlike radical terms

number theory

numerator

percent of increase/decrease

product

properties of the Real numbers

proportionality/direct variation

quotient

radical

radicand

real numbers

scientific notation

simplest form

variable

Algebra

acute angle	inequality
adjacent side/angle	integer
algebraic equation	integral coefficient
algebraic expression	integral exponent
algebraic fraction	integral root(s)
analyze	intersection of sets
axis of symmetry	interval notation
binomial	lead coefficient
coefficient	legs of a right triangle
common base	line parallel to the x- or y-axis
complement of a subset	linear equation in one variable
coordinates	linear inequality in one variable
cosine	literal equation
dependent	lowest terms fraction
difference of two perfect squares	monomial
element	multiplication property of zero
equation	opposite side/angle
exponent	parabola
exponential growth and decay	parallel
expression	polynomial
factoring	product
fractional expression	properties of exponents
greatest common factor (GCF)	proportion
hypotenuse	Pythagorean theorem
independent variable	quadratic equation

quantitative

quotient

ratio

relation

right angle

right triangle

root(s) of an equation

roster form

set

set-builder notation

sine

slope

solution set

subset

sum

system of linear inequalities

systems of linear equations

tangent

translate (from verbal to symbolic)

trigonometry

trinomial

undefined

union of sets

universal set

variable

verbal expression

verbal sentence

vertex

x-axis

y-axis

Geometry

absolute value function

angle

area

axis of symmetry of a parabola

circle

coefficient

cylinder

decagon

exponential function

function

generalize

geometric shape

graph of a relation

hexagon

investigate

nonagon

octagon

ordered pair

parabolic function

parallelogram

pentagon

perimeter

polygon

quadrilateral

quarter-circle

rational coefficient

rectangle

rectangular solid

regular polygon

relation

rhombus

roots of a parabolic function

sector of a circle

semi-circle

spatial reasoning

square

surface area

trapezoid

triangle

vertex

visualization

volume

Measurement

appropriate unit

conversion

cubic unit

error

linear measure

linear unit

magnitude

measurement system

rate

relative error

square unit

unit

Statistics and Probability

appropriateness

biased

bivariate

box-and-whisker plot

calculated probability

categorize

causation

central tendency

complement

conditional probability

correlation

cumulative frequency distribution table

cumulative frequency histogram

data

dependent events

dependent variable

element

empirical probability

experimental design

extrapolation

favorable event

finite sample space

five statistical summary

frequency distribution table

histogram

independent events

independent variable

interpolation

line of best fit

linear transformation

maximum

mean

measure of central tendency

median

minimum

mode

mutually exclusive events

not mutually exclusive events

percentile rank

probability

qualitative

quantitative

quartiles (specifically: first, second, third or lower, middle, upper)

range

sample space

scatter plot

series

univariate